VGM Opportunities Series

OPPORTUNITIES IN
ADULT EDUCATION CAREERS

Blythe Camenson

VGM Career Horizons
NTC/Contemporary Publishing Group

331.7

C 181ad

Library of Congress Cataloging-in-Publication Data
Camenson, Blythe.
    Opportunities in adult education careers / Blythe Camenson.
        p.   cm. — (VGM opportunities series)
      ISBN 0-658-00108-6 (cloth). — ISBN 0-658-00109-4 (pbk.)
      1. Adult education—Vocational guidance—United States.
    2. Continuing education—Vocational guidance—United States.
    I. Title. II. Series.
    LC5219.C24   1999
    374'.023—dc21   99-37763
                                               CIP

Cover photographs: © PhotoDisc, Inc.

Published by VGM Career Horizons
A division of NTC/Contemporary Publishing Group, Inc.
4255 West Touhy Avenue, Lincolnwood (Chicago), Illinois 60712-1975 U.S.A.
Copyright © 2000 by NTC/Contemporary Publishing Group, Inc.

Printed in the United States of America
International Standard Book Number: 0-658-00108-6 (cloth)
                                                  0-658-00109-4 (paper)
      01 02 03 04 LB 18 17 16 15 14 13 12 11 10 9 8 7 6 5 4 3 2

DEDICATION

I would like to dedicate this book to Ellen Raphaeli,
adult educator, lifelong friend, and big sister.

CONTENTS

   The main areas of adult education. Job settings. Deciding
   your area of specialization. Working conditions. Training.
   Job outlook. Salaries. Help with the job hunt.

   Personal enrichment. Skills upgrading. Salaries in adult
   continuing education. Firsthand accounts.

   Differences between adult basic education and adult remedial
   education. ABE and literacy programs. ESL programs. GED
   programs. Citizenship programs. Employment settings. Job
   outlook. The qualifications you'll need. Firsthand accounts.

   Vocational-technical education and the law. Job settings for
   vocational-technical education. Job outlook. Duties of the

voc-tech and prebaccalaureate instructor. The qualifications
you'll need. Firsthand accounts.

The different types of counselors. Key components of
successful counseling programs. Participants and settings.
Opportunities for career and vocational counselors. Working
conditions. Advancement opportunities. Job outlook.
Salaries. Firsthand accounts.

Job titles and duties. Working conditions. Employment
figures. The qualifications you'll need. Advancement
opportunities. Job outlook. Salaries. Firsthand accounts.

ABOUT THE AUTHOR

A full-time writer of career books, Blythe Camenson's main concern is helping job seekers make educated choices. She firmly believes that with enough information, readers can find long-term, satisfying careers. To that end, she researches traditional as well as unusual occupations, talking to a variety of professionals about what their jobs are really like. In all of her books she includes firsthand accounts from people who can reveal what to expect in each occupation, the upsides as well as the downsides.

Camenson's interests range from history and photography to writing novels. She is also director of Fiction Writer's Connection (FWC), a membership organization providing support to new and published writers. FWC's website can be found at http://www. fictionwriters.com.

Camenson was educated in Boston, earning her B.A. in English and psychology from the University of Massachusetts and her M.Ed. in counseling from Northeastern University.

In addition to *Opportunities in Adult Education Careers,* Blythe Camenson has written more than four dozen books for NTC/ Contemporary Publishing Group. She has also co-authored with Marshall J. Cook, *Your Novel Proposal: From Creation to Contract* (Writer's Digest Books, 1999).

FOREWORD

Across the United States and Canada adult students are going back to school. The reasons for this are numerous: employees are finding themselves downsized, skills and the technological knowledge necessary for many jobs keeps changing, older learners wish to continue to better themselves, adults with disabilities refuse to be idle and unproductive, to name but a few.

Over the years, the number of adults furthering their education continues to grow. Therefore, this field offers expanding opportunities for teachers of adult education. In this book, you will find a broad range of experiences as expressed by people working in this area—how they came to the field of adult education and why they stay. One or more of the stories you read about here may resemble your own.

Are you excited by the idea of teaching adults who have come to you with a desire to learn? Are you relieved not to have to deal with the discipline problems and lack of interest that younger students—who are forced to go to school—sometimes present? Would you like to help people turn their lives around using their new knowledge and skills that you have taught them? If so, then you will find this book a tremendous aid in planning your career as an adult education teacher.

The Editors
VGM Career Books

ACKNOWLEDGMENTS

I would like to thank the following professionals for sharing information about their work and providing insights into the world of adult education careers:

Claire Best, ESL Instructor
Cheryl-Lani Branson, Social Worker/Student Advocate
Judy Burns, Continuing Education On-line Instructor
Jean Campbell, GED Counselor
Pat Carroll, Educational Medical Consultant
Karen Carver, Computer Lab Instructor
Marshall J. Cook, Writing Professor
Joy Davis, Basic Skills Instructor
Rosemary Day, English Instructor
Adele Fuller, Career Counselor
Lynn Goodwin, Tutor/Student Literacy Coordinator
Phyllis Hanlon, Business Writing Instructor
Barbara Hogue, Cosmetology Instructor
Sheila Levitt, GED Instructor
Bernard LoPinto, Correctional Facility Education Supervisor
Geraldine Mosher, Computer Instructor
Ellen Raphaeli, Associate Professor, English
Gail Rubin, Aerobics Instructor

Louise Tenbrook Whiting, Continuing Education Court-
  Mandated Courses
Terry Thompson, Computer Learning Center Coordinator
Debi Violante, Assistant to the Supervisor of Adult Education

CHAPTER 1

THE ADULT EDUCATION FIELD

More people are realizing that lifelong learning is important to success in their careers and to their overall satisfaction with life in general. An estimated four out of ten adults participated in some form of adult education last year. To keep abreast of changes in their fields and advances in technology, more adults are taking courses for career advancement, skills upgrading, and personal enrichment, spurring demand for adult education teachers. This demand continues to rise and provides many opportunities for those entering the adult education field. Predictions are that this field will grow faster than the average of other fields, up through at least the year 2006.

THE MAIN AREAS OF ADULT EDUCATION

Adult education teachers instruct in three main areas—adult continuing education; adult remedial education, also known as adult basic education; and adult vocational-technical education, which also includes prebaccalaureate training and training for college credit.

In addition, adult education programs utilize the skills and services of career and vocational counselors and program directors and other administrators.

Adult Continuing Education

Adult continuing education instructors teach courses that students take for personal enrichment such as cooking, dancing, exercise and physical fitness, photography, writing for publication, and finance, to name just a few.

Other instructors help people update their job skills, maintain licenses, or adapt to technological advances. For example, an adult education teacher may provide courses that will help keep a health professional's skills current, or train students how to use new computer software programs.

Courses also can be mandated by courts or other bodies of law or offered by community service organizations and cover such topics as drunk driving, domestic violence, suicide prevention, crisis intervention, AIDS prevention, teen pregnancy prevention, gambling and other addictions, and financial management to help offenders stop writing bad checks.

Adult Basic Education

Adult basic education teachers provide instruction in basic education courses for those who need to improve their literacy skills, for those who did not complete high school and are studying to take the General Educational Development examination (GED exam), or for others who need to upgrade their skills to find a job. Within this category are also teachers of English to speakers of other languages (TESOL) and those who provide instruction for citizenship classes.

Adult Vocational-Technical Education and Prebaccalaureate Training

Adult vocational-technical education teachers provide instruction for occupations that do not require a college degree, such as welder, dental hygienist, paramedic, x-ray technician, auto mechanic, and cosmetologist. They also work in junior or community colleges, providing students with prebaccalaureate training and training for college credit.

Other adult education teachers help students upgrade their skills so they can reach the level necessary to be allowed into an academic program. Often these precollege courses do not offer college credits but are, instead, a prerequisite for admission.

In addition, some four-year colleges and universities offer extension programs with credit-bearing courses that are taught by adult education instructors.

Career and Vocational Counseling

Students working to achieve high school equivalency, acquire new job skills, or upgrade existing skills often take advantage of the services of the career or vocational counselors their program provides. These counselors help students identify the skills they have, coupled with their interest areas, and then pinpoint possible career paths they would be suited to. Counselors can also help job candidates improve their resume-writing and interviewing skills.

Adult Education Administration

Just as with any work setting, in the adult education field administrators are needed to plan programs, supervise instructors and other staff members, schedule classes, oversee staff meetings, and take care of finances and budgeting.

Some administrators may also interact with other community agencies to identify needed services and the different populations they will serve. They might also write grant proposals or participate in fund-raising events to finance their programs.

JOB SETTINGS

Adult education teachers work in a variety of settings. They are employed by public school systems; community and junior colleges; four-year colleges and universities; businesses that provide formal education and training for their employees; automotive repair, bartending, business, computer, electronics, medical technology, and similar schools and institutes; language centers; jails and prisons; the military; dance studios; health clubs; job training centers; community organizations; parks and recreation centers; labor unions; computer on-line services; and religious organizations.

DECIDING YOUR AREA OF SPECIALIZATION

The field of adult education is very diverse and many adult educators already have mastered a particular skill area or specialization before deciding to seek employment within the many adult education settings available. For example, a professional writer already accomplished in the field, might decide to share her or his knowledge and help other people achieve the same status. Once that decision has been reached, the task is not to study the different areas of specialization and choose any particular one, but only to locate the most appropriate job setting. Will she or he teach in an adult continuing education program held at a community college or perhaps in an on-line campus? A professional cosmetologist might, for example, after many years in the field, decide to change gears and teach others the profession in a voc-tech institution.

For those just starting their own university training and who desire to teach, the choices of specialization within adult education are much wider and not limited to the field already accomplished in. Does the future instructor prefer working with students who require basic education skills such as reading and math, or would he or she prefer working with students from overseas, upgrading language skills necessary to enter college?

For those pursuing a master's degree in counseling as a profession, the adult education option is as viable as mental health counseling, school guidance counseling, college counseling, or any of the other many counseling majors.

Although administrative positions within adult education programs are often filled from within, there are also advanced degree programs that prepare candidates specifically for roles within adult education administration.

Future adult educators, counselors, and administrators can make their choice of the path to follow based on their own interests and skills, the amount of training necessary to reach their goals, and the job availability predicted in the various areas. Whether starting out in another profession, then entering adult education, or choosing adult education as the end goal, the future adult education specialist has choices that are numerous and can be professionally and personally rewarding in each area.

WORKING CONDITIONS

Of the approximately 560,000 adult education teachers employed nationwide, most work part-time, teaching one or two courses in the evenings or on the weekends.

Most full-time adult education instructors generally work in the vocational-technical end of adult education. Some full-time workers are also employed by community colleges.

To accommodate students who may have job or family responsibilities, many adult education courses are offered at night or on weekends and range from two- to four-hour workshops and one-day minisessions to semester-long courses.

Because adult education teachers work with adult students, they do not encounter some of the behavioral or social problems sometimes found when teaching younger students. Unless court mandated, the adults are there by choice and usually are highly motivated—attributes that can make teaching these students rewarding and satisfying.

However, teachers in adult remedial education deal with students at different levels of development who may lack effective study skills and self-confidence, and who may require more attention and patience than other students.

Some adult education teachers have several part-time teaching assignments or work a full-time job in addition to their part-time teaching job, leading to long hours and a hectic schedule.

Although most adult education teachers work in a classroom setting, some are consultants to businesses and teach classes at the job site.

TRAINING

Training requirements vary widely by state and by subject. In general, teachers need work or other experience in their field and a license or certificate in fields where these usually are required for full professional status.

In some cases, particularly at educational institutions, a bachelor's, master's, or doctoral degree is required, especially to teach courses that can be applied toward a four-year degree program.

In other cases, an acceptable portfolio of work is required. For example, to secure a job teaching a flower arranging course, an applicant would need to show examples of previous work.

Most states and the District of Columbia require adult remedial education teachers to have a bachelor's degree from an approved teacher training program, and some require teacher certification.

Some school boards, such as those providing GED training or counseling, require their instructors to have a master's degree.

Adult education teachers update their skills through continuing education to maintain certification requirements, which vary among institutions. Teachers may take part in seminars, conferences, or graduate courses in adult education, training and development, or human resources development, or may return to work in business or industry for a limited time.

Businesses are playing a growing role in adult education, forming consortiums with training institutions and community colleges and providing input to curriculum development. Adult education teachers maintain an ongoing dialogue with businesses to determine the most current skills required in the workplace.

Adult education teaching requires a wide variety of skills and aptitudes, including good communications skills; the power to influence, motivate, and train others; organizational, administrative, and communication skills; and creativity.

Adult remedial education instructors, in particular, must be patient, understanding, and supportive to make students comfortable and to develop trust.

Some teachers advance to administrative positions for school boards, in departments of education, for colleges and universities, for government funded community agencies, and in corporate training departments within private business. Such positions may require advanced degrees, such as a doctorate in adult and continuing education.

JOB OUTLOOK

Rising demand for adult education courses for career advancement, skills upgrading, or personal enrichment and enjoyment will spur faster-than-average employment growth; opportunities should be best for part-time positions.

Many job openings for adult education teachers will stem from the need to replace people who leave the occupation. Many teach part-time and move into and out of the occupation for other jobs, family responsibilities, or to retire.

Opportunities will be best in fields such as computer technology, automotive mechanics, and medical technology, which offer very attractive, and often higher paying, job opportunities outside of teaching.

SALARIES

Although teachers rarely bring home huge salaries, you can expect to earn a respectable living in adult education. Salaried adult education teachers who usually work full-time have median earnings around $33,500 a year. The middle 50 percent earned between $20,000 and $46,000. The lowest 10 percent earned about $14,000, while the top 10 percent earned more than $60,000.

Earnings vary widely by subject taught, academic credentials, experience, region of the country, and the budget of the hiring institution.

Part-time instructors generally are paid hourly wages—usually from $15 to $50 an hour or more—and do not receive benefits or pay for preparation time outside of class.

Full-time adult education personnel generally receive benefits such as health insurance, paid vacations, and sick leave.

HELP WITH THE JOB HUNT

If you have an employer in mind for whom you'd like to work, a phone call or an introductory letter sent with your resume is a good way to start. Some organizations such as adult education centers or community colleges have telephone job hot lines, that are updated regularly with current openings.

If you would like some more ideas on possible job settings and how to approach them, there are several professional associations listed in the appendix that can lead you to interesting destinations. Many of these professional associations produce monthly or quarterly newsletters with job listings.

But don't overlook the obvious. Many positions are listed weekly in your local newspapers' classified section.

In addition, adult education positions at universities and colleges are often announced in the *Chronicle of Higher Education,* a weekly periodical with a large employment section. It is available through libraries or by contacting:

Subscription Department
    Chronicle of Higher Education
    P.O. Box 1955
    Marion, OH 43305

CHAPTER 2

ADULT CONTINUING EDUCATION

Adult continuing education can be divided into two major sectors: personal enrichment and skills upgrading.

PERSONAL ENRICHMENT

Adult education instructors teach courses that students take for personal enrichment. This can be anything from aerobics to writing poetry, from raku pottery to ethnic cooking. The list is only limited by your imagination. Look at any adult continuing education catalog to see the wide range of offerings.

Personal enrichment instructors don't necessarily have to have any particular degree but, of course, they are usually proficient in their field. A pottery instructor, for example, must be an accomplished potter and also must have the ability to teach others. A writing instructor should have a portfolio of published work. In other words, those who can, do, and those who can, also teach.

Some areas, though, do require certain licensing or certificates. For example, a SCUBA instructor should be trained and authorized by a certifying body such as PADI or NAUI.

Employment Settings for Personal Enrichment Courses

Settings where you'd find personal enrichment courses include universities and colleges offering evening adult education programs; vocational-technical schools with adult evening programs; adult education and community centers; health centers, hospitals, and rehabilitation centers; recreation organizations such as the YMCA; Internet services such as America Online; and even some jails or prisons.

SKILLS UPGRADING

For some professionals to stay current in their fields, their employers may require a certain number of continuing education units each year. These are usually taught by trained professionals who are licensed by the state. For example, someone providing continuing education to nurses should also be a trained nurse.

In addition, some students take courses on their own to upgrade their skills so they can be promoted on the job or land a better job. Courses could range from how to use a particular computer program to improving business writing skills. These courses are taught by instructors with expertise in the particular areas.

Employment Settings for Skills Upgrading Courses

Settings include those mentioned above for personal enrichment courses as well as at corporate offices, where businesses might directly employ instructors to work with their personnel.

In a corporate setting corporate trainers teach communications skills between staff and management, conduct seminars and workshops, run motivational sessions, and teach new skills and upgrade existing ones.

A corporate trainer could work with employees and a new computer system or provide orientation to new employees. The role of the corporate trainer can be as varied as the company's enterprises.

In addition, there are several centers nationwide providing computer training services for people with disabilities. These people either have been disabled from birth or face dealing with a new disability that, in most cases, forces them to switch careers. Disabilities range from general back injuries, for example, which force a wallpaper hanger to change jobs, to very severe disabilities, in which someone has use of only one finger or is so paralyzed that she or he needs to blow through a puff stick to be able to type.

SALARIES IN ADULT CONTINUING EDUCATION

Salaries vary widely, depending on the hiring organization and the area of the country in which you might be employed. Some personal enrichment instructors are paid hourly—anywhere from $10 to $50 an hour. Others are paid a percentage of the registration fee per student. This could range from $15 to $50 or more, depending on the type of course or the organization offering it. The more students you attract, the better your salary. Some employers might require a minimum number of students, though, before the instructor would be able to teach the class.

Some corporations keep full-time instructors or trainers on staff and pay them an annual salary. In general, salaries in private corporations are higher than those in educational institutions. A corporate trainer with a few years' experience could expect to earn $50,000 a year or more.

FIRSTHAND ACCOUNTS

What better way to learn about a profession than from specialists working directly in the field. The firsthand accounts that follow in this chapter cover adult continuing education classes conducted by a self-employed health professional; classes held in a four-year university; classes sponsored by a state district attorney's office; classes offered by an on-line campus; classes offered through the YMCA; classes held in a vocational-technical high school; and classes offered through a computer training center.

Pat Carroll—Educational Medical Consultant

Pat Carroll teaches continuing education programs for the health professions. She is owner of Educational Medical Consultants, based in Connecticut. Her work takes her all over the United States.

Carroll has a number of degrees including an A.A.S. in respiratory therapy, an A.S. and B.S. in nursing, a B.S. in health sciences, and an M.S. in education. She started her work in this field in 1983.

GETTING STARTED

"I have loved teaching since I lined up my stuffed animals and played 'school' when I was six years old. I have always loved to learn and subscribe to more than thirty journals so I can keep up on the latest information in health care. It was a natural step for me to take my love for learning new information to sharing it with others.

"My training was mostly on-the-job. There are seminars for health professionals who want to give seminars, but I pretty much did it all on my own.

"I started out my career as a respiratory therapist. But, I was always interested in nursing. I subscribed to a nursing journal when I was in RT school so I could learn more. After reading the journal for a year, I realized they didn't have many good articles about respiratory patients, so I wrote one. It was well received, so I wrote more. Then I went to nursing school. A company that put on nursing seminars saw my articles, called me up, and asked me if I wanted to travel around the country and give seminars.

"I have owned my own business now for thirteen years. Before I started my own business, I worked in the hospital as a respiratory therapist and a nurse. I enjoyed doing the seminars, but found it hard to keep a regular hospital job and travel at the same time.

"I took a job teaching in a program for medical assistants at a business school. It was only twenty hours a week, so that gave me the chance to start building my own business at the same time.

"Through my articles, I began to get calls from medical manufacturers who wanted to know if I did consulting work. Even though I didn't, I said yes, and was hired to design educational programs for them. When a company comes out with a new product, they need to train the nurses and other health professionals who will use the device, so that's where I came in. I don't sell the product—that's very important. I just provide education about the condition for which the product was designed and how the product is used for that condition.

"After two years, my side business had gotten busy enough that I stopped teaching and built the business full-time.

"Now, through my writing and teaching, I have a national reputation. I speak at national conventions for nurses and health professionals, and that's how new clients get to know me."

WHAT THE WORK IS LIKE

"I am an educational consultant hired by hospitals, medical manufacturers, pharmaceutical companies, and colleges to provide continuing education to people who work in the health professions. My students are people working as nurses or in other health fields such as respiratory therapy, radiologic technology, and physical therapy. They take my courses to keep up with new advances in medicine so they can take better care of their patients.

"Some professions require this type of continuing education after people graduate from college; some states require the courses in order to hold a professional license. So, some people come to my courses because it is required; others come because they want to learn new things and be as up-to-date as possible.

"When a client asks me to develop an educational program, I ask them what it is they think the nurses (for example) need to know to understand the product (or drug) and use it safely. Then, I do a lot of research. I go on the Internet and look for articles that have been published about the same topic. I need to be an expert in the area before I can give an educational program.

"From the Internet, I get only the author, title, and name of the journal where the article is published. I have to go to the library and find all the articles. Then I have to read them and study them to understand all the information.

"After I have done all the research, I write an outline of what I want to teach. I review that with the client to make sure nothing is missing. Then I design slides that I will use while I give my presentation. The final step of the planning process is to write a summary that is copied and given to each person who attends the seminar. That's how they take the information home. We call it a handout, and it has the summary of all the information and a complete list of all the articles I reviewed on the topic.

"Then, I usually have to travel to a different city to give the presentation. Sometimes it is close to Connecticut, where I live; sometimes I have to fly across the country to California. I usually arrive the day before the seminar. I check the room where I will be speaking to see what it looks like and if it is set up properly. I try to go to bed early and get a good night of sleep, but I don't always sleep well in the hotels.

"The next day, I get to the room early before I speak. I double- and triple-check everything to make sure there are no problems. Then I greet people who come for the seminar. Finally, I do the presentation, and afterward, I meet with people who have questions or want more information. Then, it's usually off to the airport to go home.

"I speak for audiences as small as fifty and as large as one thousand. The rest of the time, I do office work. I spend a lot of time with e-mail and on the Internet, because that's one way I keep up with new advances. There is a lot of paperwork required. My clients need it to make sure the educational programs I design are high-quality and not sales pitches for products or services.

"I work on average about sixty hours a week…usually six days. I work in an office in my home when I am not traveling. I try to work as an ER nurse one evening a week; I spend about fifty hours a week on my consulting business."

THE UPSIDES

"I would never use the word boring to describe what I do. I am on the cutting edge of new advances in health care and am always learning new things. I can't imagine a better job. I love the fact that I am there when brand new drugs and devices are being developed. I get excited about these interesting new things, and I love sharing that excitement with the people who come to hear me speak."

THE DOWNSIDES

"The downside is the travel. I have been doing it now for sixteen years, and it isn't glamorous. A lot of people think it is, but most people who travel on business don't like it very much. I go to a lot of the same cities over and over. And, while I love what I do, I would like to work fewer hours. I think almost anyone who is self-employed struggles with the same dilemma."

SALARIES

"The earning power is all over the map. Less experienced health professionals just starting out can make $50 per hour; other, more experienced nurses who are well known can make $2,000 per day. It is very, very individualized, and a lot of it depends on whom you work for. When I do programs for a local community college, I get $25 per hour for classroom teaching. When I worked full-time in the emergency department as a nurse, I made $28 per hour. Overall, I make about the same amount of money as I would if I were a nurse executive in a hospital or other agency, about $58,000 a year."

ADVICE FROM PAT CARROLL

"To teach adults, the most important thing is to understand that the process is very different from teaching children. A lot of people who don't understand that are not successful. You have to understand that adults need to know why they are learning something. You should also strive to involve people in what they are learning so they will remember things better.

"If you want to teach adults, you need to know your subject matter well. It is most helpful if you have life experience that you can bring to your teaching. Adults learn best if you can help them solve problems, and many times you can do that best by relating your own experiences. That's why I maintain a clinical practice as an ER nurse myself."

Marshall J. Cook—Professor, University of Wisconsin, Madison

Marshall J. Cook is a full professor in the department of communication programs within the Division of Continuing Studies at the University of Wisconsin, Madison. He is also a writer with hundreds of articles to his credit, a couple of dozen short stories, and numerous books including *Writing for the Joy of It, Freeing Your Creativity, How to Write with the Skill of a Master and the Genius of a Child, Slow Down and Get More Done, Leads and Conclusions, Hometown Wisconsin,* and *Your Novel Proposal: From Creation to Contract,* which he co-wrote with this author, Blythe Camenson.

GETTING STARTED

"I have a B.A. in creative writing from Stanford and an M.A. in communications/print journalism, also from Stanford. I went to law school for about four months, and I was teaching one class at the University of Santa Clara in California. I realized I didn't want to be a lawyer. I liked studying the law but not the actual different jobs lawyers do, so I bailed out of that.

"At about that time one of the teachers at Santa Clara died and I got his job; they hired me full-time. I worked there four years in the English department.

"It was like an old dream had been reborn. Ever since I was a kid the only two things I really wanted to do were to teach and write. And now I've found something that lets me do both—which is really nice. I got the class at Santa Clara basically just to make a few bucks to put myself through law school, and I discovered I really liked it. I don't think I was really that good at it at first, but it really appealed to me.

"I came to the University of Wisconsin in 1979 as a member of the academic staff as a program coordinator. I'm probably the last person in the system who came in this way, but at that time you could move from the academic staff track to what they call a tenure track. So I moved into being an assistant professor, which is a professor without tenure. Then I put in my requisite five to six years and applied for tenure at the associate professor level. Once you hit that rank, it's with tenure. Another three years after that I applied and became a full professor."

WHAT THE WORK IS LIKE

"Most of what I teach is noncredit—continuing education units only. I do teach two credit courses through our independent learning correspondence program: News Writing and Feature Writing.

"My job is really wonderful, and it's very different from the traditional campus teacher. The Division of Continuing Studies is a separate division within the university, and our primary mission is adult education. I do a lot of workshops and some consulting and some on-site training of newspaper people, corporate communicators, and a variety of other people. For example, I run media workshops for cops called 'preparing to be interviewed by the press' and one on newsletters that I've done for sixteen years. Another workshop is on stress management, and it follows the title of my book, *Slow Down and Get More Done.*

"Basically, I offer anything we can sell to the public. We're an income-generating unit, unlike campus teaching, and we're responsible for paying our own way.

"I develop the workshops and help publicize them and teach them, too. I'll personally teach maybe sixty to seventy of these a year, along with guest speaking and speaking at some conferences and helping at other conferences.

"I teach much more than the average professor in a university, but there's no research component to my job. My research is all practical, and my publications are all mass media, because that's what I teach."

THE UPSIDES

"It's diverse—one of those rare opportunities to combine writing with another career that feeds the writing rather than detracting from it. The writing helps me teach and the teaching helps me write."

THE DOWNSIDES

"It's very stimulating, but it can be enormously tiring. I do a lot of traveling, mostly within the state, bringing the workshops to where the people are. We have down times, around Christmas or in the summer, but we do have busy seasons, too, and when it's hot, it's hot. Sometimes I have to do three workshops in a week. I have to be careful not to overschedule myself."

ADVICE FROM MARSHALL J. COOK

"These days to become a full professor on a tenure track, you'd need to get your Ph.D. and it should be in a field you have some passion for.

"It's a wonderful thing if you get the chance to do it, because you not only deal in ideas, but you get to share them and watch them grow as you interact with young minds that aren't nearly as trained as yours, but are flexible and hungry for the knowledge you have."

Louise Tenbrook Whiting—Adult Educator

Louise Tenbrook Whiting teaches a class called Checks & Balances, designed for the first-time offender and sponsored by the Orange County District Attorney's office in Southern California as part of their Bad Check Restitution Program.

She has also taught courses on crisis intervention, suicide prevention, and domestic violence.

Whiting has a B.A. in psychology and an M.A. in counseling psychology and has been in the field since 1979. She has participated in numerous training programs including: suicide prevention/intervention, crisis intervention training, domestic violence, child abuse, rape crisis counseling, elder abuse, spousal abuse, alcohol and drug abuse and intervention, assertiveness training, communication training, hot line training, grief counseling, and courses in teaching adult education.

GETTING STARTED

"My first related job was working on a hot line. I answered a classified ad in the newspaper that stated: 'Help Wanted—Office Manager to work with volunteer employees.' The person on the telephone refused to reveal anything about the job; I was to learn more at my first interview at a woman's house—not in an office.

The woman was a well-known community leader and I knew I had nothing to fear.

"During the interview I was told I would be managing a crisis intervention/suicide prevention hot line at a secret location. I would also be hiring, firing, and supervising volunteer help. When I questioned the location of the hot line office, I was told I would be given that information only if I was hired for the position. After a second interview, I was hired, but I was still not given the office location until the evening before I was to report for work. All of this 'cloak and dagger' intrigue and secrecy was appealing to me, and I was very excited about my new 'mystery' management position.

"Working on the hot line, I learned many things and came in contact with people I had only seen on the evening news. Due to the nature of some of the calls, there were occasions when the FBI and the local police were conferring in my office. Although we were in Southern California, it was also during this period that Ted Bundy, the serial killer, had not yet been apprehended. He was a former volunteer of a Seattle, Washington, hot line. I read everything I could about him and carefully scrutinized our volunteers.

"I frequently read the classified ads for my local newspaper online. I am always looking for something that looks interesting, challenging, and just a bit different from what I have done in the past. I do look for something where I can use my license or my skills. The job teaching the bad check class sounded different, and the ad read 'will train.'

"Many job ads give no name, address, or telephone number— only a fax number; this was one of them. I quickly updated my resume and faxed it as requested. About a week later I received a phone call. There were two telephone interviews, then one in-person interview, and I was hired.

"I was given a training manual and worked closely with experienced teachers. I observed their teaching/training techniques and then did some co-teaching before going on my own."

WHAT THE WORK IS LIKE

"I teach an eight-hour class called Checks & Balances to a group of students who are legally required to be there. A merchant (most commonly places such as Target, Kmart, Wal-Mart, and supermarkets) files a formal complaint. The District Attorney is obligated to follow up. People come into this class two ways, although both are court mandated.

"The first way is if a person is a first-time reported offender. They have the option of attending the class in lieu of going to court. This is a misdemeanor charge.

"The second way is if the person goes to court and then is still ordered to take the course. Many people have written more than one bad check, but a lot have only one. The reason might be they have no reserve or overdraft for their account. When the first check bounces and the penalties are charged, it may cause a domino affect and other checks start bouncing. When a person goes to court they may they be required to pay $350 to $400 per check, plus community service hours, and one-year summary probation. Or, they may be able to take the class in lieu of that. Most people opt for the class.

"The people coming into the class are common everyday people just like you and me. They are not bad people or necessarily bad check writers. The problem is that for the most part they live paycheck to paycheck, juggling their bills and trying to survive. In this class they are taught life skills that, when followed, will hopefully prevent this from happening in the future.

"If they fail to attend, a warrant for their arrest could be issued. It is also my responsibility to have the students fill out a registration form and sign into the class. At the end of the class, each student completes an evaluation form and receives a certificate of completion that I have made out and signed. This certificate can be presented to the court when needed. At the end of the day, I have a report to complete. I then return all paperwork to the office for their record keeping.

"Students come into class with mixed emotions. Some are angry, irritated, or hostile. Others are feeling embarrassed or humiliated. One thing they all have in common is none of them wants to be there! They have all kinds of preconceived ideas as to what the class will be like and the kind of people who will attend. None of them expect it to be the way it is, and for the most part they are pleasantly surprised. As the class begins, though, I am definitely not the most popular person in the world.

"During class, my initial goal is to get the students to lighten up, relax, and not expect eight hours of being berated for having bounced a check. I open with a humorous story or anecdote, all the while praying for at least some laughter. I'm a good storyteller and this usually happens. I use the story to illustrate some of the feelings they may be experiencing at the moment. Whatever their early responses are, I keep the class moving until I observe they have become responsive.

"Everyone then introduces themselves and relates what happened that brought them to class. I make sure the environment is caring and supportive. The students are no longer strangers and realize that they all have a lot in common—and, more importantly, that none of them is 'bad.'

"Throughout the day I use humor, by what I say or what I do. We cover a variety of topics, from basic bookkeeping/check balancing skills to taking control and making positive life changes. I emphasize appropriate values, attitudes, and behavior.

"The work is interesting because each time I teach the class it is to a whole new group of people. Some reactions and responses are the same, yet I hear or learn something new every session.

"Bounced checks may come from direct deposits being late or an urge for Rocky Road Ice Cream, to a four-cent miscalculation. There are a variety of reasons, some are laughable, some are sad, however, they are never boring.

"I work hard to make the class an informative, interesting, and rewarding learning experience. I also try to make it as enjoyable as can be expected. I would say 99.9 percent of the evaluations indicate that I am succeeding.

"My relationship with each student is short-term, though, and I never see the results. Often, I can see where further training or intervention is warranted for some, but at the same time, I know my job has ended and I must let go.

"This is a part-time job and I have chosen to work one day a week. It is considered an eight-hour class, however, my day is much longer. When the day is completed, I may review the course materials during the week. Also, I like to do research on-line regarding finances, investing, money management, wealth, and prosperity. These are areas covered in class, and I want to be current and knowledgeable.

"Because of my background with crisis intervention, suicide prevention, domestic violence, and counseling, I was also able to teach a domestic violence/spousal abuse class. This class is also court mandated, geared toward offenders who have been charged with a felony. This is a totally different population from the bad check class, and students can be from all different socioeconomic levels, from the corporate executive to an unemployed laborer. The common denominator is violence. For the most part they are angry, hostile, and don't want to be there.

"I have taught this group in a hospital setting because most of the time they are also drug abusers and/or alcoholics. Their charges may be lessened by opting for treatment.

"But the people in the class will try to sleep through the meetings or become angry and leave. If it is at all possible to break the shell with some, progress may be made. However, the prognosis is not the best. It is usually better to deal with the spouse or significant other and encourage them to make the necessary life changes.

"What I teach is something that should have been learned in childhood. Because the violent behavior is so ingrained, by the time a person ends up in a program, they may have no desire to change. It is challenging and definitely needed, yet it is also stressful and potentially dangerous."

SALARIES

"The salary for any of these types of classes is usually on a per-class basis and not hourly. The earnings vary based on whether you are self-employed or working for someone else. When working for a company with an established program, the salaries are not as high as you would earn independently. However, the companies have an established client base and assume all costs and responsibilities."

ADVICE FROM LOUISE TENBROOK WHITING

"Educate yourself first. For teaching in some of the areas I mentioned above, a degree might not be required. Depending on your experience, however, it would certainly lend credibility. Take classes or training in your area of interest, do research, and read everything current you can find on the subject.

"Do volunteer work where you will receive training and hands-on experience. It is important to your own future and well-being to experience both the best and worst aspects of this type of work. The more education you have, the more doors it will open.

"Volunteer to speak or do training for groups in your community. Become known for your expertise.

"Learn both speaking, training, and writing skills. You may be called on to write programs and then teach them."

Judy Burns—AOL On-Line Instructor, Screenwriting

Judy Burns teaches Introduction to Screenwriting on America Online in its Online Campus. She is a writer-producer-story consultant whose extensive prime-time credits include *Star Trek* ("The Tholian Web"), *MacGyver, Stingray, Airwolf, T. J. Hooker, Magnum P. I.,* and *Cagney and Lacey.*

She also teaches screenwriting at UCLA Extension, Ithaca College, UC Riverside, and other universities around the country.

WHAT THE WORK IS LIKE

"On-line education can come in a couple of ways. You can teach for a university or for an on-line service. UCLA Extension, for instance, now offers about seven classes on-line. These classes are actually taught via e-mail because UCLA doesn't have an Internet server that allows for IRC, Internet Relay Chat—a virtual classroom people can actually use on-line.

"Basically, the university courses are more like correspondence courses but they pay the instructors very well, maybe $1,200 or $1,300 for ten weeks for fifteen students. Through AOL you get maybe $15 to $30 per student.

"The course I teach on AOL is divided into three parts. Part one consists of learning how to create or find a story, pitching the idea, the story spine, introducing and developing new characters, using mythological archetypes, and writing a story outline.

"Part two looks more closely at story structure, character motivation, subplots, setups and payoffs, development of tension and conflict, and writing the beat outline—the blueprint for a feature film screenplay.

"Part three consists of formatting the script, writing professional dialogue and narrative, scene and sequence construction, getting your script into a marketable form, and presenting it to agents and the industry.

"It's very energizing teaching on-line. You have the same dynamics in an on-line classroom that you would have in a standard classroom, except that it might be a little more controlled. Off-line you can look them in the eye, and off-line they also have a tendency to bounce around in the class a bit. On-line you don't know if they're bouncing around. What you do know, is that if you're getting their attention and getting them interested, they will start to really chatter at you. I stop my lecturing and ask them to count off and let me know what they're thinking, and they respond resoundingly.

"The only disadvantage is that they have to go look at the films outside the classroom. Normally I would show a film in a standard class and talk about it at the same time we watch it.

"There's another thing I've found that's a little different. In a standard classroom I can tell everybody that what we say in the classroom stays there. For everyone's protection we have to agree not to steal someone else's idea. I tell them, if you're not comfortable with that, then please go away. What I found on-line was a reluctance on the students' part to put their material out until we had been on-line together for about ten or fifteen weeks. By the tenth week, they knew each other and began to post their material. On-line it takes longer to build up trust—you can't see people's eyes."

GETTING STARTED

"It was something I was interested in. I knew they must be teaching classes on-line, so I went on-line and found the Online Campus on AOL. I knew there were actual universities running on-line classes, so I figured AOL would be, too.

"I was looking for the experience of teaching on-line. I investigated it myself. I'm computer literate and knew it was out there. My co-teacher and I made a proposal and the coordinator accepted it.

"I started in August 1995 offering a free class. New instructors on AOL have to give a freebie class first so the coordinator can make sure they're comfortable with the environment."

ADVICE FROM JUDY BURNS

"It's easier if you design your course so you're teaching in lecture mode rather than in workshop mode. With a workshop you spend more time dealing with students' work, and unless it's a very lucrative teaching position, at a university, for example, where they charge regular university tuition fees, it's not cost-effective.

"If you want to teach on-line, go to the World Wide Web, call up a search engine for educational institutions, and then look to see if they are carrying courses on-line. If so, you could then send an e-mail to the person in charge of the program with your resume and a proposal to teach on-line.

"In terms of services, AOL is the best—there's not much in the way of classes on the other services. But another way is to do it yourself, by setting up a home page.

"You would need a small working knowledge of how computers function. For example, you have to know the speed of your modem and the fact that information gets transferred faster the larger the number. If you have a slow modem it takes longer and will ultimately cost you more."

Gail Rubin—Aerobics Instructor

Gail Rubin is a full-time public relations professional, but she also teaches aerobics part-time at the YMCA of Greater Albuquerque. She started her work there in 1998.

GETTING STARTED

"I have a B.A. in communications from the University of Maryland, College Park. As an aerobics instructor, that doesn't mean much, although I do have to communicate well with the class.

"I enjoy keeping fit and had attended step aerobics classes for about three years when I decided I'd like to teach aerobics. Years before, I had attended water aerobics classes and had an opportunity to fill in for the teacher a couple of times. I've always liked working up a sweat, leaping around to music, and teaching aerobics is a fun way to do that *and* get paid for it.

"I noticed a steady turnover of aerobics instructors at the Y where I took classes, and I asked my instructor about the possibility of becoming a teacher. She said the aerobics coordinator was just starting a training class to prepare for an expected wave of turnovers (one teacher was pregnant, one was planning to move to another state). She said if I was really interested, I should go through the training and after I took the certification classes, I could start teaching. And that's what I did.

"The training for YMCA instructor certification is provided by the organization. I took two weekend training classes and trained for three months to learn cuing, choreography, stretching, and building a routine.

"Most health clubs require additional certification from other organizations. Additional classes are required to maintain certification for both Y and health club teaching. All aerobics instructors are required to have current certification in CPR and first aid, which I got through Red Cross classes."

WHAT THE WORK IS LIKE

"The classes I primarily teach are held during weekday mid-mornings, so the majority of my students are older women, although two older men regularly show up. Their goals include getting or staying fit, losing weight, and improving flexibility, blood pressure, and heart rate.

"As a low-impact instructor at the YMCA, my duties include:

1. Setting up the room for class—bringing music and setting up the stereo, making sure the room is safe for aerobic activities (the floor is clean, comfortable temperature), having students sign in an attendance logbook.

2. Leading the class through warm-up, stretching, aerobic conditioning, muscle conditioning, cool down, and stretching.

3. Observing the students for any health problems during the class and responding appropriately with assistance as needed.

4. Keeping the aerobics program coordinator informed of any planned absences and arranging for a substitute teacher.

"Aerobics instructors have a reputation for being chirpy and cheerful, and you need a certain amount of that kind of sunny personality to charm your class, cheerlead them to work their hardest, and keep them wanting to come back. One woman who was a fellow classmate in my step class took the instructor training course. I was surprised to see her training to teach, because she was very quiet and shy. She started teaching the early morning step class that we both used to take, but the class slowly dwindled down until no one showed up. That class was finally canceled. She just didn't have the personality to pull people in so early in the morning.

"I like getting up in front of my class, chatting with them as we stretch, throwing in goofy comments now and then. My routine doesn't change that much, but I gradually work in different moves just so folks don't go on total autopilot (including myself).

"With the same people coming week after week, you find out a bit about their lives outside the gym. Some ask for information about exercise or diet, and I provide them with the best answers I can.

"I teach three regular classes—Monday, Wednesday, and Friday—an hour and fifteen minutes each. Sometimes I'll fill in for other aerobics instructors in the evening or substitute teach the muscle toning class.

"Teaching aerobics is not my main source of income. It is just a part-time endeavor with some great benefits. I work out of my home as a public relations professional/writer, take a break midmorning to teach my class, come home and shower, and get back to the better-paying PR work.

"The management of aerobics instructors at the YMCA is pretty minimal. As long as you show up on time, provide an upbeat class, keep the attendance log, and clock in and out, outside of a meeting every month or so, we are solely responsible for our classes.

"One of the benefits of being an instructor at the YMCA is automatic membership, which at the club where I teach is worth about $250.

"I travel for my PR work to Washington, DC for extended periods of time, and I also applied to be a substitute aerobics instructor in that area. As a part-time employee, I have access to their wonderful facilities. This includes indoor swimming pool, fitness equipment, many aerobics classes, sauna in the locker room, and free towel service. If I use the facilities as a visiting YMCA member from another town, I would have to pay $7 per visit. And you can write off costs for aerobic shoes, music, clothes, and equipment on your taxes."

THE UPSIDES

"I get paid to work out! I feel great after work. I like to know that my students have had a good workout. I enjoy saying to people, 'Why, yes, I am an aerobics instructor.' "

THE DOWNSIDES

"I have to work out on a regular schedule, and I can't just not show up because I'm not in the mood to exercise. The class depends on me to be there. It's hard on your body to teach more than one class a day.

"The pay is not that great, but it's better than nothing. I get paid on an hourly basis. I started at $9.50 an hour. With more experience at this particular facility, I could get up to $12 an hour. Private health clubs in Albuquerque pay up to $21 an hour, but you need more training and certification than the Y requires. In the Washington, DC YMCA, the starting pay was $11.50 an hour, ranging up to $21 an hour for more experienced, specialized teachers."

"If you want to be an aerobics instructor, you've got to have an almost cheerleaderly personality. If you're not motivating your students, they will not show up for class.

"Also, you've got to be in pretty good shape to start with. You've got to enjoy music and movement and people. You can't be afraid to make a fool of yourself now and then. You've got to learn the basics of teaching aerobics, which you can investigate either through a local YMCA or health club. They should be able to refer you to training classes. (Costs for those classes vary widely.)

"Learn to teach a range of aerobics—low/high impact, step, spinning—and you'll be much more marketable than if you just know one type."

Phyllis Hanlon—Business Writing Instructor

Phyllis Hanlon teaches business writing in an adult evening program held at Bay Path Vocational-Technical High School in Charlton, Massachusetts. She began freelance writing in 1997 and started teaching in 1999.

GETTING STARTED

"I graduated from the Salter School/New England School of Accounting in September 1993 with a medical secretarial diploma. I entered the job force, moving from the medical world to a non-profit art organization.

"I began continuing my own education as an evening adult student in 1996. I received my associate degree in liberal studies (summa cum laude) in May 1998. In December 1998 I completed requirements for a communications certificate on a business track. In the fall of 1999 I received a communications certificate on a creative track. I am presently about ten courses away from obtaining my bachelor's degree. All of these educational accomplishments took place at Assumption College in Worcester, Massachusetts.

"I became a certified aerobics instructor in 1986. From that time until June 1998 I taught a variety of fitness classes in area facilities.

"I have been writing for magazines and newspapers for the past two years. I have also edited newsletters and other written communications as part of my own business.

"I am a board member and secretary for the Society of Professional Communicators. Through this group I have been exposed to many experts in the field of communications. I have attended workshops and seminars that have strengthened my skills and introduced me to new ones.

"For several years I taught religious education classes to first and third graders as well as junior high school students. Using my dance background, I also taught members of my church (both children and adults) liturgical dance.

"Since returning to school in 1996 I have never been happier with my life. Apparently I am one of those people who could be a perpetual student. My academic background prepared me well for the corporate world where I had worked as an administrative assistant for various managers. During my years as an assistant, I had the opportunity to compose and edit numerous letters. Some of this written communication dealt with vendors, other business people, and organizations. I wrote solicitation and late payment reminder letters, among others. When upper management began asking me to create the letters without their assistance, I realized that I had a knack for this type of activity. My grammar and punctuation skills have always been strong. Where others labored over a simple letter, I attacked the job with joy and finished the task quickly.

"Once I left the corporate world and began my own freelance writing career, I saw an opportunity to help others by teaching one of my own strengths. I had no formal training for this position. My confidence in the subject and willingness to share the information with others have given me the impetus to teach. The other teaching experience I received from my church and the exercise activities prepared me somewhat for the present job. Even though the subject matters are all quite different, the basic classroom setting is the same.

"In November 1998 a local vocational-technical high school advertised for teachers for their evening adult education classes. Since I had been mulling over the possibility of teaching a business writing class, I jumped at the chance the ad presented. I wrote a proposal, outlining the areas of business writing that I would cover in the class, and submitted it to the director.

"The director of the night school program contacted me when she received my letter. We spoke about the proposal and finalized the deal.

"In addition to completing requirements for my bachelor's degree, I have inquired about a teaching certificate. I do like teaching at this level, though, and do not need to have a certificate for that."

WHAT THE WORK IS LIKE

"I teach in an adult evening school situation. My class runs for seven weeks. The students do not get college credit but can receive a certificate of completion if necessary for tuition reimbursement by their employers or for their own personal use.

"The school is a vocational-technical high school, but the classes for the adults at night range from computer topics to dancing.

"This term I had only women in my class. They all hold full-time jobs with various companies. The first night I taught I asked the students the reason for their presence. Two of them said their bosses had seen the catalog, circled the business writing class, and placed it on their desks with the 'strong suggestion' they take the class. One woman is interested in improving her grammar and punctuation skills. Another one finds she can't concisely say what she wants. She is looking for a way to streamline her writing. Still another wants to write memos and letters for her boss without getting them back 'all covered with red pen marks.'

"The class I teach is business writing. I developed the curriculum and have only five students in the class. Even though I had been teaching aerobics for many years, I was a little nervous for the first business writing class. I had about three months to prepare for classes. During those weeks I created an outline for the class, typed up class lessons and handouts, and organized a curriculum. Since this class is a noncredit, evening class, I did not want the students to have to buy a book. By making my own handouts I figured the class would have enough hands-on activities to learn the skills I was trying to teach.

"I must say that I put a lot of time into each class. In fact, I still review the agenda each week and usually add comments, worksheets, or extra lessons. My biggest fear is running out of topics or areas to discuss. It is better to have work left over.

"Before I began any of the preparations for the classes, I spoke with a writing teacher I had in college. She was a wonderful resource for me. She provided a workbook designed for teachers and gave me some hints that have been very useful. Between the book she gave me and the two that I already had, I have been able to compile in-depth worksheets that reinforce each lesson.

"Our particular classroom is just the right size to accommodate the group. I like to stand or walk around when I teach so I can make eye contact with the students and make them feel comfortable. I emphasize the 'fun learning' aspect of the course. I don't want anyone to feel pressured or uncomfortable. Everyone is at a different level regarding grammar and punctuation skills. I try to work on all the issues that concern the students.

"At the beginning of the first class, I distribute a questionnaire with demographic questions on it. I also ask the students to indicate the areas they would like me to address. In addition, I ask them to keep their eyes open for any business communications— letters, memos, e-mail—that are noteworthy for their clear, concise message or for their jumbled confusion. I feel that real-life examples are best to work with.

"I teach a two-hour class one night a week. I am considering applying to other area night school programs in the future. Since I now have the curriculum developed, the bulk of the work has been done. A seasoned teacher told me that the first time teaching the course I would be nervous; the second time I would be a little more comfortable; the third time out I would feel secure. I think she is right.

"During the day I still pursue my own marketing communications business. I meet with clients, write brochures and articles, and work on other assignments. My involvement with a professional organization also keeps me busy and current with industry trends. In my day-to-day activities, I keep my eyes open for material I can use in my classes."

THE UPSIDES

"I enjoy every aspect of my job as a part-time business writing teacher. Since I am basically a student at heart, I enjoy the preparation. It feels like my own 'homework.' It is very gratifying to develop my own class activities and feel I am giving something to these students.

"The school I teach in is very close to my home, so that is another bonus. The students themselves are interesting and fun to work with. Being adults, they are concerned with job advancement and top performance in their present positions. I am happy to think I can influence them and their accomplishments in the workplace. At this point I cannot see any downsides to the job."

"The school where I teach pays $18.50 per hour for classes. The payment is made in one lump sum at the end of the semester."

ADVICE FROM PHYLLIS HANLON

"If you are considering teaching, you should think about your favorite types of activities. Have you been involved in some academic area or some other activity for a long time? Do you feel the skill you possess is strong? Could you talk about this subject in your sleep? If you are that comfortable in some area, then that is probably your starting point.

"Also, you need to consider your own personality type. Would you be able to explain this activity or subject to a group of strangers? Do you have a fear of speaking in public? You must consider your own comfort level. Having the knowledge and being able to impart it are two different things.

"If you do not possess a teaching certificate and have not been involved in a teaching role before, the easiest way to begin a teaching career is in an adult education program at a local high school or community college. Typically the classes are noncredit, which relaxes the restrictions on teachers. As long as you are sure you can communicate a subject you know well and love to your students, I would encourage you to try. The experience can be very uplifting and exciting. When you provide information that will strengthen an existing skill or introduce a new one, the satisfaction you receive is tremendous."

Karen Carver—Computer Lab Instructor

Karen Carver worked for Independence, Inc. in Lawrence, Kansas, an independent living center providing computer training to disabled people. She functioned as a lab instructor and the center's webmaster. She started her work there in 1985 and finished in the spring of 1999.

GETTING STARTED

"I use a wheelchair, and the idea of helping others to learn something that could aid them in their search for employment was appealing. In 1983 I started as a student with the program I now work for. I became well acquainted with the staff from taking classes through them. When a position opened up I applied and was hired. That was in December of 1985. I began to learn new software from more classes I took and on my own so I could teach them."

WHAT THE WORK IS LIKE

"The students are disabled adults ranging from high school age to someone over eighty years old. Disabilities range from mild to severe to terminal. The main goal of most of the students was just trying to overcome the fear that they couldn't operate a computer! Once they found out they could, they'd then quite eagerly take the next step of learning the programs more in-depth. What they chose to learn was up to them, as long as they'd had the basics beforehand or could prove basic ability if they didn't want to take a beginning class.

"Many came in with the desire to learn so they could gain working skills. And as long as they stuck to the program, they received such skills. There were also those who came in to learn only word processing so they could type letters at home. Some came to learn spreadsheets so they could do their own financial statements. One lady who had reached retirement age wanted to learn Lotus so she could keep track of her and her husband's business. I tried to steer her to more simplified software, but she had an old computer that already had Lotus on it, so that's what I had to teach her.

"Some students are sent to us from the Vocational Rehabilitation Department. These are students who want to take computer science through college or vocational-technical schools. The VocRehab sends them to us to take them through at least one class. In this way, the agency knows the student can handle the computers and it can deal with them through higher education.

"Some students want to learn computers merely so they can play games! Yes, we have a few games, but we do try to discourage people from spending hours on them in the lab. It takes up space from those who wish to learn software for work. Also, if too many want to play games at once, it gets much too noisy!

"Some students can't afford computers at home, so they come in to do work for school. This is accepted also, as long as they have some type of disability.

"Some come in to keep up their typing skills while looking for a new job. And, I believe, there are a few who keep coming back for the socializing with the other people there. The students cover absolutely every aspect of society. So we meet some very interesting people!

"I started off teaching, but now I mainly work on the center's website. When I was teaching classes, I sometimes had an assistant, but often I was on my own. Sometimes I would have up to thirteen students on a computer at a time. Classes generally last one hour. I usually only taught one class a day. I worked from 8:00 A.M. to 12:30 P.M., four days a week, and 5:00 P.M. to 7:30 P.M. one night a week. When I wasn't teaching a class I was working on material for the next day's class, while also assisting consumers who weren't in structured classes. They could come in during time when classes weren't scheduled and work on anything they wished.

"This meant I could have anywhere from one to a dozen people that I was responsible to assist by myself while trying to do my own work for the next day, plus go over any paperwork handed in.

"I taught Introduction to Computers, which is a basic class for people who had never touched a computer before, or had very little experience on computers. It covers everything from what keys do what on the keyboard to explaining all the buttons and lights on the computer. It also covers how to hook up your own computer and how disks store information. I also included the very basics of DOS for those who had old computers.

"Then I'd provide an introduction to word processing, databases, and spreadsheets, using the following programs: WordPerfect, Word for Windows, Excel, Access, Dbase III +, DOS, Lotus, Windows. Other courses covered the Internet, and two were on basic troubleshooting. One was very basic, such as checking the cord to make certain the machine was plugged in or connected tightly to the machine if it didn't turn on. I also taught a much more comprehensive troubleshooting class.

"I also had to be a good troubleshooter in my job. If something went wrong with the computer or software, I had to hope to fix it quickly.

"As an instructor I was responsible for preparing lessons. This might mean preparing hard copy handouts or disks for certain classes. During class I would provide examples, and then I'd give out exercises for the next class. We were also responsible for 'grading' our own classes, documenting students' progress.

"I was also responsible for coming in one night a week to help students who weren't able to utilize the lab during the day. Some nights would be full, and once in a while, no one would show. There weren't any fixed schedules because we wanted people to feel the lab was available as they needed it.

"Some of the computer systems use different versions of Windows. Some of the computers turned on differently. The different style of computer systems would sometimes confuse people. Independence, Inc. is a nonprofit organization, so the computer lab—known as the CLC or Computer Learning Center—only gets new computers when funding is available. We also only get whatever model we can find at the best price at that time. As a result, we have many models, although all are IBM compatible. Very few students were mentally challenged, yet most seemed to have a considerable amount of trepidation when it came to touching or operating the computer.

"In addition to teaching classes, all of the instructors are available for one-on-one training with students during hours when classes aren't in session. Even when I had an assistant, we might still get bogged down, trying to keep people in step with others. It seemed that no matter how much we screened people to try to place those with equal ability in the same class, we would usually wind up with one or two who would have great difficulty keeping up, and a few who were as fast as lightning.

"Of course nothing is perfect. There are, and always will be, times when one of us doesn't know an answer or can't fix a problem. We then rely on another instructor or the administrator, Terry Thompson. (See his firsthand account of administering this program in Chapter 6.)

"We are constantly updating software and fixing any computer or software problems. We also review and change teaching plans as needed and make class changes as needed. At the end of each course we ask what the students would like to see taught next. This enables us to keep up with what our consumers are interested in. We also send out yearly surveys to businesses to see what type of software they utilize so we're teaching what is used in the community.

"In February 1998 I began a different venture at the lab, working on the website. I was able to work from home. At first I just entered their newsletter on the Internet and processed data to keep track of the number of people who used the lab and went over lesson plans. Later, they wanted a trivia website, and wanted me to do it. I knew nothing then about html and they didn't want to use a page publisher because many servers don't accommodate them.

After many frustrating months of learning through trial and error, the site is just about ready. Because the site has to be accessible to people with different disabilities, I had to create two versions, one with graphics and one with none."

THE UPSIDES

"I like the contact with people and the various personalities. I also like having access to all the different software I can't afford myself.

"The best part, though, is when, after a long period of frustration, that light finally goes on in someone's head, and they take off and figure out how to do things. It's also very rewarding finding out that someone who had only a GED landed a well-paying job because of their computer skills."

THE DOWNSIDES

"We never seem to be able to keep up as well as we'd like. We never have enough help during classes. Another large problem is being unable to keep as current with the computer world as is necessary because of financing problems.

"And it can get frustrating if someone quits a class because they believe they'll never learn. Of course, it's impossible to have a 100 percent success rate, but that doesn't keep us from trying. It also doesn't keep us from feeling that we've personally failed the person who leaves, even though it really isn't our fault."

SALARIES

"I was paid $7 an hour for a twenty-hour workweek."

ADVICE FROM KAREN CARVER

"You need a large amount of patience. If you have little to no patience, then this isn't the job for you. Many people with disabilities have self-esteem problems, and they don't need mistreatment from someone who can't take time to help them without making them feel guilty. Don't assume that just because a person is disabled he has no knowledge, or that he is mentally challenged just because he's computer illiterate.

"Also, because you'd be largely on your own, you need a wide knowledge of the computers and software being used. If a program locks up—or the computer—you need to find the problem and, hopefully, save the project the student is working with."

CHAPTER 3

ADULT BASIC EDUCATION

Adult education teachers who instruct in adult basic education (ABE) programs—also known in some settings as adult remedial education—may provide adult literacy training; teach adults reading, writing, and mathematics up to the eighth-grade level; teach adults through the twelfth-grade level in preparation for the General Educational Development examination (GED); or work with students who do not speak English.

ABE programs can also provide support to developmentally challenged students to live and work more independently by studying personal/home management, communication, computation, reading, writing, and life skills. In addition, ABE programs can focus on teaching students citizenship skills.

Finally, some adult remedial education programs—also known by the preferred term of developmental programs—are provided at junior colleges, technical-vocational schools, and community colleges to bring students up to the standard required for admittance into credit-bearing courses toward a degree or certificate. This area of adult education is covered in Chapter 4.

DIFFERENCES BETWEEN ADULT BASIC EDUCATION AND ADULT REMEDIAL EDUCATION

Although adult basic education and adult remedial education sound the same, there are some distinct differences. The major difference between the two is the skill level of the student. Students whose skills fall in the grade one through five level—below the sixth grade level—on a college entrance exam (all colleges and universities, all fields of education—especially developmental—use the sixth grade level as the independent level, especially in reading) are considered unable to function on an independent level in reading, math, or English. Those students are not admitted to a technical college without first enrolling and succeeding in ABE courses to bring up their skill levels.

Adult remediation courses, now mostly known as developmental courses, are designed for students who can function independently (seventh grade and above) but whose test scores on the college entrance exam indicate that their abilities in math, English, or reading need strengthening before they can take the courses required to complete their certificates, diplomas, or associate degrees.

As in all colleges, placement in math, English, or reading classes is determined by scores made on the ASSET entrance exam.

ABE centers are federally funded and located at many facilities in each state. They are separate from colleges and universities. Community colleges legally cannot teach ABE courses, since ABE courses are tuition-free and also offer no credit. (For more information on developmental courses taught at community colleges and technical schools, see Chapter 4.)

ABE AND LITERACY PROGRAMS

Literacy helps individuals continue to learn new information, read for pleasure, read newspapers to be informed about the world and their communities, handle everyday tasks, and be independent and take care of their own needs.

Literacy is also important to allow older people to remain in or rejoin the workforce or to contribute to society through volunteerism and civic participation.

Many factors help explain why so many adults demonstrate English literacy skills in the lowest proficiency level. Many are immigrants who have not yet learned to speak English. Others have terminated their education before completing high school. Others have physical, mental, or health conditions that keep them from participating fully in work, school, housework, or other activities.

As part of their workload, adult education teachers prepare lessons and assignments, grade papers and do related paperwork, attend faculty or professional meetings, and stay abreast of developments in their field.

ABE teachers may refer students for counseling or job placement. See Chapter 5 for more information on adult education counseling.

Because many people who need adult basic education are reluctant to seek it, teachers also may recruit participants.

Sample Literacy Job Listing

A County Library is seeking an experienced adult literacy specialist to work at the library's Second Chance Program. This is a part-time, 15 to 20 hours a week, temporary position.

The successful candidate will primarily be responsible for student support activities that will include: providing workshops and experiences for the students to promote the development of personal advocacy and leadership skills; offering computer-assisted learning and instruction in the use of the Internet; tracking and recording student achievements, including the development and implementation of an 'exit interview' questionnaire; assisting with student recruitment and volunteer training; and supervising part-time student advocates. Must be available some nights and weekends.

Minimum Requirements: Valid driver's license required. Possession of a baccalaureate degree with a major in education, psychology, communications, humanities, social science, or a closely related behavioral science field.

Experience: One year of full-time or its equivalent experience in adult literacy programs or as a certified teacher of educationally or economically disadvantaged groups.

Substitution for Education: Additional qualifying experience of the type noted above may be substituted for the required education on a year-for-year basis up to a maximum of four years.

The selection process includes an application and an interview.

ESL PROGRAMS

It's estimated that more than one thousand million people around the world speak or are studying how to speak English. They choose to learn English for a number of reasons: to attend colleges and universities in English-speaking countries, to ensure better business communications, to enhance employability, to facilitate government relations, to create a more rewarding travel experience, or, for many, to be able to communicate day-to-day in the English-speaking country in which they live.

In the United States alone, a recent study revealed that more than 2.5 million non-native English speakers with limited English proficiency enrolled in U.S. public schools, grades K through twelve. This figure is a 68.6 percent increase from previous years.

Enrollment in adult programs during the same period was reported at approximately 1.2 million, a 40 percent increase from the previous available figures.

It is safe to assume that the demand for English instruction around the world also will continue to rise. This means many opportunities for instructors who are interested in living and working outside of North America.

Sample ESL Job Listings

English as a Second Language, one (1) 2-year term renewable instructorship. Duties: Teach ESL for academic purposes; assist in ESL curriculum development/research. Required: M.A. in TESOL or equivalent; 2 years' teaching experience overseas or in intensive English program. Salary: $28,500 (minimum) plus benefits for academic year. Summer employment is possible. Send letter of interest, CV, 3 letters of reference.

Position: ESL High School Teacher. Duties: classroom instruction. Requirements: valid state secondary credential authorizing ESL or bilingual instruction. Qualifications: appropriate student teaching or equivalent. Salary: $27,526–$46,737. Benefits: health, dental, and vision insurance. Starts: August.

Private language institute in Japan. Position: Instructor. Duties: Teach approximately 20 periods per week in either intensive business course or nonintensive course; some administrative and residential responsibilities. Qualifications: M.A. in TESL plus two years' experience, or appropriate experience in business or international relations. Location: Nice small city one hour from Tokyo, near mountains and sea. Salary: 329,000 yen per month to start, with a raise each year. Benefits: Travel paid in arrears, seven weeks paid vacation, numerous others. Starts: Summer.

International Language School in Madrid. Position: ESL Instructor. Duties: plan, teach, and evaluate assigned classes according to established curriculum. Requirements: 30 hours/week with split shift possible. Contract: 9-month. Qualifications: Native English speaker, B.A./B.S. degree plus 1-year full-time ESL teaching experience or degree in TESL/TEFL. Preferences: advanced degree in TESL/TEFL plus 2 years ESL experience. Salary: 137,000 pesetas/mo. Benefits: Round-trip airfare, medical coverage, paid vacation, sick leave, and on-site orientation.

GED PROGRAMS

The General Educational Development (GED) tests give adults sixteen and older who did not graduate from high school the opportunity to earn a high school equivalency diploma. The GED diploma is recognized nationwide by employers and educators and has increased education and employment opportunities for millions of adults since 1942.

The GED was developed and is administered by the General Educational Development Testing Service. More than 750,000 adults each year take the GED exam. About one out of every seven people who receive high school diplomas each year earns that diploma by passing the GED tests.

The GED Testing Service contracts with nearly 3,500 official GED testing centers in the United States, Canada, and overseas to provide test materials and to monitor services to examinees. The GED testing program is jointly administered by the GED Testing Service of the American Council on Education and each participating state, provincial, or territorial department or ministry of education.

Sixty-five percent of GED test takers plan to enter a college, university, or trade, technical, or business school during the year following the test. The average age of people taking the GED exam is 24.7. More than 95 percent of employers nationwide employ GED graduates on the same basis as high school graduates in terms of hiring, salary, and opportunity for advancement.

The adult education programs of most school boards provide classes to help students prepare for the GED battery of tests.

Instructors work with a curriculum found in most secondary schools—English, math, science, social studies, and history.

School boards with GED programs also hire qualified people to administer the tests. In addition, many counselors opt to work with GED test takers to help determine career goals upon completion. (See Chapter 5 for more information on GED counseling opportunities.)

Sample GED Job Listing

County School Board seeks qualified GED instructors for adult education classes held at satellite community centers. Qualifications: bachelor's degree and state high school teaching certificate. Hours: 25 to 30 hours a week. Half day on Saturdays. Duties: prepare adults from the age of 16 for the GED exam. Must be able to work with a wide range of subjects: language usage, reading comprehension, math, science, and social studies. Salary: $19 an hour, $24 an hour with a master's degree.

CITIZENSHIP PROGRAMS

Although there are exceptions, applicants for naturalization must be able to read, write, speak, and understand words in ordinary usage in the English language. Applicants for U.S. citizenship must also have a knowledge of U.S. history and government.

Sample Job Listing for Citizenship Classes

Position: adult educator for citizenship preparation classes offered by the university continuing education program. Must possess a bachelor's degree and be certified to teach high school or adults. Hours: 12 hours per week, Monday–Thursday,

7 to 10 P.M. Salary: $15 per hour. Benefits: discounted tuition for university courses. Free parking. Starts: immediately.

EMPLOYMENT SETTINGS

Most jobs in adult remedial education, including ABE, ESL, GED training, and citizenship classes, are provided by city and county school boards. School board sponsored classes can be held in public schools during the evening hours, in local community centers during the day, and some ABE and GED programs are available in hospitals and prisons.

Teaching English as a second language (TESL) often falls into the category of ABE, and the job settings are more varied for this particular aspect. In addition to evening ABE programs through the public schools, you can find ESL classes on the campuses of community colleges and four-year colleges and universities, in private language schools, and also as part of the regular curriculum in the primary and secondary grades.

JOB OUTLOOK

Enrollment in adult remedial education programs is increasing for a number of reasons: More employers are demanding higher levels of basic academic skills—reading, writing, and arithmetic. This spurs the demand for remedial education and GED preparation classes. There is also an increased awareness of the difficulty in finding a good job without basic academic skills.

Also, changes in immigration policy and citizenship requirements mandate a basic competency in English and civics.

A recent survey by the U.S. Department of Education's National Center for Education Statistics estimated that about 21 percent of the adult population—more than forty million Americans over the age of sixteen—had only rudimentary reading and writing skills. Most adults at this level could pick out key facts in a brief newspaper article, for example, but could not draft a letter explaining an error on their credit card bill. A subgroup in this category—representing roughly 4 percent of the total adult population, or about eight million people—was unable to perform even the simplest literacy tasks.

What does this all mean? The number of people in the United States desiring ABE, GED, and ESL instruction is on the rise. As public school systems, government agencies, and private enterprises continue to work toward filling the demand, opportunities for ABE and ESL teachers will continue to grow.

THE QUALIFICATIONS YOU'LL NEED

Qualifications for many ABE and GED positions are usually the same for any teacher working in a public school system: a bachelor's degree and a teaching certificate.

At one time, it was believed that the only qualification necessary to teach English to non-native speakers was to be a native speaker yourself. But these days that school of thought has almost vanished. Before the TESOL profession had firmly established itself as an important and valid discipline, an individual could venture overseas, finding teaching work along the way to cover travel costs and living expenses. Although such situations, tutoring and part-time teaching, do still exist in a few locations, they are quickly shrinking, replaced with quality programs touting qualified and experienced ESL teachers, both at home and abroad.

Most ESL teachers have bachelor's degrees; those working in community colleges and four-year institutions often have master's degrees.

FIRSTHAND ACCOUNTS

The firsthand accounts that follow in this chapter include a student literacy coordinator and tutor, an ESL instructor, and a GED instructor.

Lynn Goodwin—Tutor and Student Literacy Coordinator

Lynn Goodwin works as a student literacy coordinator for Project Second Chance, a program offered through Contra Costa County in California. She is also a volunteer tutor there and at the Sylvan Learning Center and in America Online's Academic Assistance Center. She has more than twenty years' experience in high school and college education as well as four years running a private acting class.

She earned her B.A. in drama and theater at Vassar College in Poughkeepsie, New York, in 1971 and her M.A. from San Francisco State University, also in drama and theater, with a minor in community college teaching in 1982.

GETTING STARTED

"I inherited my interest in education. My mother taught English. Today she is still an avid reader. I learned so much comparing my mother to other classroom teachers. My father owned a men's retail store and helped with math homework when the need arose. School and good grades mattered to both of my parents. Education was valued in my home.

"I was attracted to teaching adults because they choose to be there, unlike adolescents serving time in public education. I thought I had ideas to offer. Project Second Chance supplied me with techniques.

"In the information age, people who cannot read signs, fill out a form, read to their children, read a note from a child's teacher, or read labels operate with a frustrating disability that also can cause great embarrassment. Often nonreaders become masters of deception. As I got older and more frustrated with the public school system, I felt a greater need to help those who fell through the cracks.

"I started off volunteering at Project Second Chance then simultaneously started tutoring for America Online's Academic Assistance Center (AAC). I know my recommendation from AAC helped me get my job tutoring with the Sylvan Learning Center. I volunteer at all three places, but have had to cut my hours since I was recently hired at Project Second Chance as a paid staff member working twenty hours a week. I specialize in making the computer rooms accessible to learners, and I function as a student advocate. Volunteering to work with adult learners can often lead to paid employment in the field.

"When I was just starting volunteering at Project Second Chance, the paid staff provided three all-day Saturday training sessions. And I rely on common sense and encouragement. I was willing to volunteer as an adult literacy tutor because I believe in giving back."

WHAT THE WORK IS LIKE

"The students (learners) at Project Second Chance are adults who read below a fifth grade level. Many have learning disabilities such as dyslexia. About a third are not native English speakers; they speak English, but have trouble reading and writing the English language. Many come to the program for personal improvement. They want to give more to their children than they had for themselves.

"My job has two focuses: improving learner recruitment and communication, as well as making the computer rooms accessible to learners.

"I have designed assessment interviews that are conducted with the learner at six weeks, six months, and upon exit from the program. This is so I can assess learner progress and address concerns. Basically, I ask the learners leaving the program questions to find out why they are leaving and what they learned.

"I am also involved with student recruitment and put out 'Learn To Read' cards at the local convenience stores and county day care centers. I contact school secretaries and adult school administrators to help spread the word. I hope to place ads on the county bus system. I find one idea or connection leads to another. I plan to invite learners to help us recruit people who need our services and at the same time offer them use of the computer room.

"I am also assessing the existing software. I send e-mails to tutors, inviting them to bring their learners and come and 'play with me' in the computer room. I will also ask them what kinds of software would enhance their students' learning. I hope, after an introduction, some learners may want to spend additional time working on the various computer programs and games. We have programs in phonics, reading, writing, math, typing, Quicken, and GED prep as well as games that tap into a variety of skills.

"My job keeps me busy. I share office space with four other people at one of the sites. At the other site, the other tutor/student coordinator works alone when I am not there.

"Paid staff at Project Second Chance tutor as well as work at recruitment, textbook maintenance, ordering, training, and other program tasks.

"I am entering uncharted territory, designing new methods of recruitment and retention, as well as looking for new approaches to make the computer rooms work. Learners have an enormous amount of failure in their lives, so I operate on the premise that there are no mistakes, only new material.

"As a tutor, my duty is to help my learner any way I can. I work on skills—getting facts, finding the main idea, recognizing supporting details. I work on writing skills. We make up spelling lists based on what the learner wants to know.

"We usually work in the back of the Antioch Library. Sometimes it is crowded with learners and tutors—other times it is private. We work in separate cubicles. Because I work with one person at a time, it is seldom boring. Besides, if I show signs of boredom, it demeans the self-confidence of my learner. Instead, I am upbeat, finding what is positive or correct, and building from there whenever possible. The growth makes the job worthwhile."

THE UPSIDES

"I love the light that goes on in a learner's eyes when understanding occurs. I like the staff's receptive attitude, I like the computer programs, and I like the people I have contacted who want to help spread the word. I like the energy that is generated by tutors and learners coming through the office. I like the feeling that the program is making a difference in the lives of both learners and tutors."

THE DOWNSIDES

"I hate the early morning calls from learners canceling our sessions. Another downside is the frustration that occurs when a learner becomes impatient with herself or himself or is easily defeated."

SALARIES

"My salary of a little more than $15 an hour is paid by a grant written by Project Second Chance's director. Salaries in adult literacy range from about $10 to about $30. If a person is a full-time school district employee, the salary will go higher."

ADVICE FROM LYNN GOODWIN

"Care about people. Learn to listen. Be creative. Enjoy creative problem-solving. Be open to what the job requires. I am venturing into new territory for this organization. Other tutors/student coordinators work mostly on intake and matching learners with tutors. They provide materials and trouble-shoot. Be prepared to train tutors. Always value volunteers. Adult learners often failed in the public school system, and you must provide individual success as well as a positive, trusting environment as quickly as possible. The traditional classroom often does not work for these learners. Even in small groups, you will need trained volunteers to assist you. Value them and they will give back. Respect and enjoy the learners who want to give back.

"There are often requests for adult literacy volunteers at any public library. Volunteering and interning are great ways to try a new career.

"To earn the credentials for a paid career, contact the education department of your local university.

"I would strongly encourage people interested in adult literacy to realize that funding is limited. Grant writing would be an additional, desirable skill."

Claire Best—ESL Instructor

Claire Best taught English as a second language to adults through an adult education program affiliated with her local school board, as well as in a private language center. She also worked overseas for many years teaching English as a foreign language to first-year university students.

WHAT THE WORK IS LIKE

"There's a big difference between teaching in the United States and teaching overseas. In the adult education program here in which I worked, my classes were filled with students from a variety of countries. Overseas, of course, the students will all be from the country you're in.

"When you're in the United States, your class is finished and you go home. Overseas, your workday might be over, but the experience of living in another country is with you every day, all day. I much prefer teaching overseas. It's far more exciting and one of the main benefits to the profession. You can work almost anywhere.

"No matter where you're teaching, though, your work is pretty much the same. You instruct students in basic English language skills: reading, writing, listening, and conversation. Like any teachers, you're responsible for designing lesson plans and for administering and grading tests. I also helped develop the teaching program and materials we used in the classroom.

"My jobs in the United States required many more teaching hours than my university jobs overseas. So you're on your feet a lot and you're talking a lot. I always lost my voice for a few days at the beginning of each new term.

"I found I preferred the administrative aspects more than the actual teaching. My last job overseas, I was a director of a program. You have to really love classroom interaction to stay with it. A lot of TESOLers get burnt out after too many years in the classroom."

GETTING STARTED

"Like many TESOLers, I just fell into it. I hadn't gone the traditional route, studying ESL; I had earned a B.A. in English but had no idea what I was going to do with it. But what I did know, or thought I knew, was that I wasn't going to teach. I also got an M.Ed., but my area of study was in counseling.

"I had been working part-time with the adult education program counseling GED students on career choices after they passed their high school equivalency, but I needed to put in more hours to make a decent living. A friend of mine was the director of the ESL evening program at one of the satellite schools, and he offered to take a chance on me. My training was all on-the-job.

"The experience I gained through adult education led me to a job in a private language program, and that led me to my first job overseas."

ADVICE FROM CLAIRE BEST

"Many people not yet in the profession think, 'I can speak English, therefore I can teach it.' In some places, that's true and, often, travelers wanting to earn extra money to help pay for their trip find work tutoring or providing practice in conversation skills.

"But as the number of professionally trained teachers increases, opportunities for unqualified teachers decreases.

"These days, a bachelor's degree is considered the minimum qualification for teaching ESL/EFL. A master's degree would be necessary to teach in a university setting. State certification as a teacher is required for those teaching in American schools and some international schools.

"Teaching English as a second or foreign language is not the same as teaching it as a first language. There is a foundation of knowledge and methodology for this field of study that includes linguistics, second language acquisition, education practices, sociology, anthropology, psychology, testing and measurement, and other related subjects.

"My advice is first to volunteer to see if this profession is right for you, and, if it is, then you should plan for your career and get that specialized training. This will open up many more jobs to you.

"The best way to find a job, especially a job overseas, is to attend the annual TESOL conference. Recruiters come in from all around the world to staff their programs."

Sheila Levitt—GED Instructor

Sheila Levitt worked with the adult education program through the school board in Dade County, Florida, for ten years, providing

GED preparation to students in a variety of settings. Sheila earned her B.A. in English and her M.Ed. from the University of Florida in Gainesville.

GETTING STARTED

"Teaching adult education was not something I had originally planned. I didn't actually have a plan when I graduated with my master's degree. I moved to Fort Lauderdale from Gainesville, and a friend suggested I contact the school board about employment. The hourly pay was not bad at the time—about $15 an hour—and what was going to be a short-term position ended up being ten years—ten years that I don't regret."

WHAT THE WORK IS LIKE

"For most of the ten years, I worked in a room in a community church that was donated to the school board. People from the community could sign up for the classes. They were free.

"My students came from all sorts of backgrounds. Some were high school age and had just dropped out of school and realized they needed a diploma. Others were older and were being encouraged to go back to school by their family members or employers. Some were just doing it for the satisfaction of making that achievement.

"I worked thirty hours a week, Monday through Friday, with an hour break for lunch. Ours was a large center, so there were two other teachers working with me. Sometimes we worked with students individually, other times we worked in groups. We had materials provided to us by the school board, and they covered all the areas the GED covers. They were arranged by levels, so, for example, we could test a new student, see what level of reading he or she had attained, and then start him or her at the appropriate level and gradually build up to more difficult material over time.

"Some students just came in for a week or two for a refresher course; others spent months preparing. The center was open from

8:00 A.M. until 4:00 P.M., and students could drop in any time between those hours; there were no set classes."

THE UPSIDES

"It was a real challenge, helping students increase their English and math skills, but very rewarding to see their improvement. When we all felt it was time for them to sign up for the test, everyone rooted for them. The best part was when a student came back to the center to let us know he or she had passed the GED. That smile and the thanks were worth everything.

"Another plus to adult education, at least in my set-up, was that we didn't have to deal with administration on a regular basis. The teachers were provided with the classroom and materials and given a free hand how we wanted to lead our students."

THE DOWNSIDES

"The only problem with this job, and it was a real problem, was that the pay was on an hourly basis. No benefits, no health insurance, no sick leave, no vacation. If you didn't work, you didn't get paid. And the thirty hours weren't guaranteed. If the number of students who came to the center dropped, your hours could be cut. There were several times I was cut to twenty-five hours for a few months at a time. That makes it difficult to budget and pay your bills."

ADVICE FROM SHEILA LEVITT

"To provide GED prep, you need the same qualities that you would for any teaching job: knowledge of the subject matter and lots and lots of patience. You have to love teaching.

"The benefits to teaching adults is that you don't have the discipline problems you'd find in a high school, and your students, for the most part, are much more motivated. If you want to teach secondary level material, but don't want to deal with the problems found in schools, adult education would be something to consider."

CHAPTER 4

ADULT VOCATIONAL-TECHNICAL EDUCATION AND PREBACCALAUREATE TRAINING

Vocational-technical education prepares students for continuing education, work, and life through the application of academic and specific occupational skills.

Traditionally, adult education teachers working in the vocational-technical (voc-tech) sector have instructed people who choose to enter occupations that do not require a college degree. These students could be high school graduates or GED holders, or they might have left high school without finishing.

The occupations that fall into the vocational-technical category cover a wide range. These are just a few examples: welder, dental hygienist, emergency medical technician, automotive mechanic, automated systems manager, x-ray technician, farmer, and cosmetologist.

But vocational-technical education is changing. It now incorporates both school-based and work-based learning and prepares participants for postsecondary education as well as employment. In fact, vocational-technical education prepares individuals for the bulk of America's jobs. In 1996, only about 20 percent of America's jobs required a four-year college degree. But many jobs require some education beyond high school, often at the community college level. For most occupations, postsecondary education is essential. Vocational-technical education now encompasses postsecondary institutions up to and including universities, providing prebaccalaureate training for courses offering college credit. Vocational-technical education also takes place within secondary schools.

Vocational-technical education allows students to explore career options and develop the skills they will need both in school and in the workplace.

VOCATIONAL-TECHNICAL EDUCATION AND THE LAW

The Carl D. Perkins Vocational and Applied Technology Education Act, Public Law 101–392, defines vocational-technical education as organized educational programs offering sequences of courses directly related to preparing individuals for paid or unpaid employment in current or emerging occupations requiring other than a baccalaureate or advanced degree. Programs include competency-based applied learning, which contributes to an individual's academic knowledge, higher-order reasoning, problem-solving skills, and the occupational-specific skills necessary for economic independence as a productive and contributing member of society.

The total appropriation for Perkins was $1.1 billion dollars in 1997. States received these funds in the form of $1 billion for their state basic grants and $100 million for tech prep. All states receive funds for secondary and postsecondary education. In 1994, Perkins provided approximately one-tenth of the total state expenditures on vocational-technical education.

According to the National Assessment of Vocational Education study, the most frequent uses of funds included: occupationally relevant equipment, vocational curriculum materials, materials for learning labs, curriculum development or modification, staff development, career counseling and guidance activities, efforts for academic-vocational integration, supplemental services for special populations, hiring vocational staff, remedial classes, and expansion of tech prep programs.

The United States competes in a global economy. The purpose of the Perkins Act is to prepare a workforce with the academic and vocational skills needed to compete successfully in a world market.

JOB SETTINGS FOR
VOCATIONAL-TECHNICAL EDUCATION

Job settings can be as varied as the different occupations the voc-tech and prebaccalaureate training sectors cover.

Vocational-technical education has an active presence within public secondary schools.

Throughout the United States there are many vocational-technical institutes specifically geared toward preparing students to enter the workforce immediately upon completion of the program.

Almost every city or county within the United States hosts one, if not more, community colleges, offering a variety of job training programs, courses for college credit, preparatory and adult education courses, as well as customized workforce training. Programs are usually two years and cover arts and sciences, business occupations, health occupations, technical fields, trades, and service occupations.

In addition, there are many private schools, such as cosmetology and beauty schools, that provide vocational-technical training in one specific subject area.

At the secondary level, there are two special programs that would be of interest to instructors considering a career in adult voc-tech education: career academy programs and tech prep education.

Career Academy Programs

Career academies are high school programs that are usually schools-within-schools—smaller administrative units operating within larger schools—that are occupationally focused. These educational structures bring together groups of students and teachers who work together over a two- to three-year period of time.

There are more than 1,100 career academies in operation, some established as long ago as the early 1960s. They prepare primarily high school juniors and seniors in such areas as environmental technology, applied electrical science, horticulture, sports education, business education, travel and tourism, aviation technology, computer engineering, avionics, building trades, and health care careers.

Career academy programs have proved to be very effective, particularly for preparing members of special populations and students seeking to enter nontraditional occupations. The career academy concept has been so successful that it is now recommended for all students who want or desire such education and training leading to existing jobs in the public and private sectors.

Career academies usually have several distinct elements that help to distinguish them from traditional education and training programs. However, it is not necessary that all of the identified characteristics be present in a particular career academy for it to be effective and provide quality education and training to all students. Individuals who graduate from a career academy program are academically and technically proficient and qualified to continue with postsecondary education or enter the labor market.

Some of the characteristics of a career academy program are:

block scheduling
reduced class size
integrated academic and vocational content
thematic learning

partnerships with business
mentoring
structured, out-of-school learning experiences

Tech Prep Education

Tech prep education is a significant innovation in the education reform movement in the United States. Tech prep was given major emphasis in the Carl D. Perkins Vocational and Applied Technology Education Act of 1990 and was amended in the School to Work Opportunities Act of 1994.

Tech Prep education is a 4+2, 3+2, or a 2+2 planned sequence of study in a technical field beginning as early as the ninth year of school. The sequence extends through two years of postsecondary occupational education or an apprenticeship program of at least two years following secondary instruction, and culminates in an associate degree or certificate.

Tech prep is an important school-to-work transition strategy, helping all students make the connection between school and employment.

The Perkins law requires that tech prep programs have seven elements:

1. an articulation agreement between secondary and postsecondary consortium participants

2. a 2+2, 3+2, or 4+2 design with a common core of proficiency in math, science, communication, and technology

3. a specifically developed tech prep curriculum

4. joint, in-service training of secondary and postsecondary teachers to implement the tech prep curriculum effectively

5. training of counselors to recruit students and to ensure program completion and appropriate employment

6. equal access of special populations to the full range of tech prep programs

7. preparatory services such as recruitment, career and personal counseling, and occupational assessment

States are required to give priority consideration to tech prep programs that: offer effective employment placement; transfer to four-year baccalaureate programs; are developed in consultation with business, industry, labor unions, and institutions of higher education that award baccalaureate degrees; and address dropout prevention and re-entry and the needs of special populations.

Student outcomes include: an associate degree or a two-year certificate; technical preparation in at least one field of engineering technology, applied science, mechanical, industrial, or practical art or trade, or agriculture, health, or business; competence in math, science, and communication; employment.

JOB OUTLOOK

Employment growth of adult vocational-technical education teachers will result from the need to train young adults for entry-level jobs and experienced workers who want to switch fields or whose jobs have been eliminated because of changing technology or business reorganization.

In addition, increased cooperation between businesses and educational institutions to ensure that students are taught the skills employers desire should result in greater demand for adult education teachers, particularly at community and junior colleges.

Since adult education programs receive state and federal funding, employment growth may be affected by government budgets.

The job market for secondary school teachers varies widely by geographic area and by subject specialty. Many inner cities—

characterized by high crime rates, high poverty rates, and over-crowded conditions—and rural areas—characterized by their remote location and relatively low salaries—have difficulty attracting enough teachers, so job prospects should continue to be better in these areas than in suburban districts.

Teachers who are geographically mobile and who obtain licensure in more than one subject should have a distinct advantage in finding a job. With enrollments of minorities increasing, coupled with a shortage of minority teachers, efforts to recruit minority teachers should intensify.

Employment of secondary school teachers is expected to grow faster than the average for all occupations through the year 2006. Assuming relatively little change in average class size, employment growth of teachers depends on population growth rates and corresponding student enrollments. Enrollment of fourteen- to seventeen-year-olds is expected to grow through the year 2006.

DUTIES OF THE VOC-TECH AND PREBACCALAUREATE INSTRUCTOR

Adult education instructors prepare lessons and assignments, grade papers and do related paperwork, attend faculty and professional meetings, and stay abreast of developments in their field.

Vocational-technical education's combination of classroom instruction, hands-on laboratory work, and on-the-job training meets students' different learning styles so all may learn.

Increasingly, adult vocational-technical education teachers integrate academic and vocational curricula so that students obtain a variety of skills. For example, an electronics student may be required to take courses in principles of mathematics and science in conjunction with hands-on electronics skills.

Generally, teachers demonstrate techniques, have students apply them, and critique the students' work so they can learn from their mistakes. For example, welding instructors show students various welding techniques, including the use of tools and equipment, watch students use the techniques, and have them repeat procedures until students meet specific standards required by the trade.

Adult education teachers may lecture in classrooms or work in an industry or laboratory setting to give students hands-on experience.

Minimum standards of proficiency are being established for students in various vocational-technical fields. Adult education teachers must be aware of new standards and develop lesson plans to ensure that students meet basic criteria. Also, adult education teachers and community colleges are assuming a greater role in students' transition from school to work by helping establish internships and providing information about prospective employers.

THE QUALIFICATIONS YOU'LL NEED

All fifty states and the District of Columbia require public school teachers to be licensed. Licensure is not required for teachers in private schools. Usually licensure is granted by the state board of education or a licensure advisory committee. Teachers may be licensed to teach the early childhood grades (usually nursery school through grade three); the elementary grades (grades one through six or eight); the middle grades (grades five through eight); a secondary education subject area (usually grades seven through twelve); a special subject, such as reading or music (usually grades K through twelve); or guidance counseling, and, in some states, adult education.

Requirements for regular licenses vary by state. However, all states require a bachelor's degree and completion of an approved teacher-training program with a prescribed number of subject and education credits and supervised practice teaching.

Some states require specific minimum grade point averages for teacher licensure. Some states require teachers to obtain a master's degree in education, which involves at least one year of additional course work beyond the bachelor's degree with a specialization in a particular subject.

For those teaching academic subjects in junior or community colleges, a master's degree is more often than not the minimum requirement, but more and more instructors are going on to earn doctorate degrees.

Many vocational teachers in junior or community colleges do not have a master's or doctoral degree but draw on their work experience and knowledge, bringing practical experience to the classroom.

FIRSTHAND ACCOUNTS

The firsthand accounts that follow in this chapter include a cosmetology instructor, an associate professor of English at a community college, an English instructor at a voc-tech institute, a basic skills instructor at a technical college, and a computer instructor at a voc-tech institute.

Barbara Hogue—Cosmetology Instructor

Barbara Hogue is a cosmetology instructor at the Arizona Academy of Beauty in Tucson. She became a hairdresser in 1974 and has been teaching for sixteen years.

She first earned her GED, then completed eighteen hundred hours of cosmetology training to become a hairdresser. After being licensed by the state board of cosmetology, she worked for several years in the field in licensed salons in Tucson. She later completed another six hundred hours of instructor's training and then was tested and licensed again by the state board of cosmetology for an instructor's license.

In addition, to maintain her accredited teacher status, she attends yearly seminars and upgrade classes on teaching techniques and the latest hair trends.

GETTING STARTED

"From the time I was a little girl, I wanted to be a hairdresser...but when I went to beauty school, I realized that my true desire was to teach as well as to do hair, skin, and nail care.

"I admired the teachers, their patience, their willingness to make learning fun. It was very far removed from any other schooling I had ever had. Each day there was something new to learn—not just book work—and I really admired the ability my instructors had and how they were so willing to help me achieve my goals. I wanted to do the same for others. It took me about ten years of working in the field before I returned to beauty school for my instructor's training, but it was worth the wait.

"Each state has different hour requirements for the initial cosmetology training and then specific requirements for becoming an instructor, over and above your initial training. But all states require expertise in the field before applying to a beauty school for teacher's training. Field experience can be as little as a year, or up to five years.

"Generally, you return to cosmetology school, enroll as a student instructor, and proceed to learn the teaching techniques set forth by the state and the federal government, if that school offers student loans or grants.

"During the teacher training time, the student instructor learns how to give lectures, use visual aids, demonstrate techniques, give detailed step-by-step instruction, create tests, keep records, perform evaluations, and do some counseling, too.

"I was hired by the school as a full-time instructor after I passed my instructor's exam and received my license. I have worked for this school on and off since 1983. Generally, a school will train instructors with the expectation of hiring them upon completion of their training and licensing."

WHAT THE WORK IS LIKE

"The school I work for runs year-round and has an ongoing enrollment. By that I mean that generally a new class can start every week, or every other week, with a rotating curriculum. The nail program starts every four weeks, not rotating, but timed so new students will be 'on the floor' by the time the senior students leave.

"'On the floor' means they get actual hands-on experience with the public, and for a very reduced price, students perform salon services. This is with any application of the cosmetology industry—hair, skin care, or nail care.

"There are basically two phases of the school: the freshman curriculum and the clinic floor.

"The freshman curriculum is a basic teaching and hands-on application (on mannequin heads for hair students or on plastic fingers for nail students). After the basic techniques are understood, the student is allowed to bring in willing patrons (friends and relatives) to practice on 'live' models.

"After this practice is done and the basic techniques are learned, the student then graduates to the next phase, which is the clinic floor, and works on the paying customers. They take appointments, create a regular clientele, learn customer service, and deal with challenging situations as they are groomed to step into a salon atmosphere. This takes hours of time. Each state has its own hour requirements.

"Also, the students must maintain an adequate work ethic and understanding of procedures under the constant supervision of an instructor.

"The instructor's job is to provide the student with the skills, both manual and emotional, to handle a wide variety of services and people. The instructor is always fully responsible for each student and his or her performance and is obligated to the customer to provide them with satisfactory service.

"Sometimes that provides many challenges for the teacher, because of varied circumstances. Some of these circumstances include personality clashes between client and student. Or the client is in a hurry and gets impatient with a slow student. Or they aren't happy with the service, and in some instances can get very nasty with the student. For some students, dealing with an angry client can be very defeating, for their confidence is shattered and they feel hopeless. A large percentage of the time, an instructor's job is to maintain a student's level of confidence, try to intervene in any situation where a client may be unhappy or impatient, while still smiling and offering the best solution for client and student.

"Some of our students might have learning disabilities, which can present difficulties for the teacher. We have to work with those specific problems to evaluate the student, but at the same time we prepare them for state testing that will not offer much leeway for the disability.

"The varied age of the students, their life experiences, their attitudes, and the creative curve are also challenging at times. In some instances, a student will be older than the teacher, which can lead to miscommunication. Plus, the older students sometimes get frustrated with the younger teenage students, and vice versa. But generally, after spending months together in the school environment, the students learn about each other and become very caring and helpful to each other. Many close friendships are formed among the students.

"A teacher's job in this is to remain neutral, try to reach all the students in a class, and move easily between one student and another constantly. For example, an instructor is responsible for twenty students plus the customers they are working on, at all different levels and phases of ability and instruction. It makes for a full day.

"I work full-time—Tuesday through Saturday—8:00 A.M. to 5:00 P.M. There is an hour for lunch, and I must adhere to my schedule as closely as possible.

"A typical day starts with a lecture in the morning, then moves to a demonstration of a technique, student practice of the demonstrated technique while being monitored, to dealing with any specific problems a student may have with that newly learned technique. This is the day's work. Constant teaching, monitoring, application and execution of one technique after another, until the student is proficient and graduated from the program.

"My grades are turned into the main office on a monthly basis, and I present each student with an evaluation (report card). Their hours are kept track of by the school and state board. I am responsible for keeping a detailed file on each student and making sure they have all the tools necessary to learn the basic applications."

THE UPSIDES

"I have always loved people, so that is what I love the most about my work. I enjoy talking to different people and helping them feel better about themselves, whether it has been a student or a client.

"It's quite an honor when someone comes to you to do her hair for her wedding or graduation or prom night or anniversary—and even sometimes because of death. Many hairdressers do the hair of the deceased, especially if the deceased was a client or relative of a client. Students become close to you over time, and I have even had the privilege to teach a second generation. To be asked to share in other people's lives is a very special honor and one that hairdressers probably get to enjoy more often than any other profession.

"Another plus is when a student happens to run into you ten years after her graduation and still remembers you—and still thanks you for making a difference in her life. That's a huge reward.

"Or watching how the young woman with several children, recently divorced, and feeling as if she had no future, can blossom and start to feel confident in herself. If you get to be a part of this successful change, that, too, is a reward.

"Or to watch a grandmother, who has always wanted to do this, but has put it off all these many years because of her family and other responsibilities—to finally recognize her goal, and you helped to make it possible, that's a reward.

"You get to make a difference by giving someone a chance to recognize her own potential and success, and when you learn she's opened her own salon, and is happy and contented with her life, you know you were a small part of something special.

"And during the time the students are in school, you are a part of their lives. You watch them graduate from high school, get married, have babies, buy a new car, re-evaluate what they want, and you watch them turn negative life experiences into positive ones. Most students never forget their cosmetology teacher—the extended learning experience is far more profound than anything they encountered in a 'regular' learning situation."

THE DOWNSIDES

"The downside is that it requires a high amount of energy on a daily basis. The job requires walking and standing and being on your feet for most of the shift. It's not uncommon for hairdressers to suffer from back trouble or leg and feet problems after years in the profession. But, much of the stress can be avoided by the use of support hose, comfortable shoes, proper diet and proper rest, and not straining the body in odd positions when doing a service.

"There is a lot of paperwork for those schools that are accredited. And to keep a perky personality and a smile going can sometimes get hard to do at times as well. But, the rewards far outweigh a long, tiring day."

ADVICE FROM BARBARA HOGUE

"If you enjoy the profession as a whole, but feel tired of working behind a chair, becoming an instructor is an ideal job. You still get to enjoy clients, utilize their own creativity, and make a difference in the lives of a lot of people. The training is generally short-term, the money is decent, and it's the perfect way to get the most out of being a people person with a caring skill.

"For a person who enjoys being busy and enjoys the variation of a daily activity, this career is perfect, for it is never boring. The pay is good, some schools offer more benefits than others, but the ongoing variety of people and keeping abreast of new styling trends and teaching techniques prevents burn-out in the profession.

"Patience, the desire to help, the desire to give, and a fairly easygoing personality seem to be a plus as a teacher. It is a people profession, and enjoying people is a must. A desire to want a student to succeed is a plus as well."

Ellen Raphaeli—Associate Professor of English

Ellen Raphaeli is an associate professor of English at Northern Virginia Community College, Alexandria Campus. She started teaching in 1964 and has taught at this particular community college since 1970. In addition, she has volunteered her time tutoring in a women's prison, has taught high school English, and has taught English as a foreign language overseas.

She earned her A.B. in English with a secondary teacher's certification from the University of Michigan in Ann Arbor in 1964 and her A.M. in English language and literature at the same university in 1967. She has done another thirty hours of graduate work toward a doctorate since being hired at Northern Virginia Community College.

GETTING STARTED

"I am a teacher by accident—not by intention. My goal from about the time I was in eighth grade was to become a psychiatric social worker. A degree in social work, however, required a two-year graduate school program. My plan was to teach for a year to save money for graduate school. I figured I could stand teaching... for a year. And then I was bitten. As soon as I got to teach my first lesson as a student teacher, I knew this was what I wanted to do.

"My first job after graduation was as a high school English teacher. Other young teachers who had been on staff two or three years would say to me, 'If you can get through the first year, you'll be fine. It gets better after that.' But I never knew what they were talking about. I already loved what I was doing.

"When, after one year's teaching, I began a graduate program, it was not in social work but in English language and literature. I also did some cognate work in teaching English as a foreign language because I thought there was a good chance my husband was going to get a job overseas.

"We left the country a year later. I didn't teach right away because I had an infant, and then two infants. But in 1968–69 I began teaching part-time—an English reading class at a university and an English conversation class at an adult education center.

"When we returned to the States in 1969, I was anxious to return to high school teaching; however, I had two toddlers and I did not want to work full-time. The public school systems were not hiring part-time teachers, but they suggested I try one of the area community colleges. I applied to two two-campus community colleges in the area (both have since become multicampus institutions). One did not hire me; the other, Northern Virginia

Community College, offered me a composition course at one of its campuses. Then I was offered a second course at its other campus. Then, after the fall term had begun, I was offered a third course to replace a teacher who had quit after the first week. I taught three courses in the fall quarter, two courses in the winter, and one in the spring. The life of an adjunct faculty member was then—and still is—fraught with uncertainties. Classes could be offered or snatched away at the last moment, and the number available to adjunct faculty dwindled between fall and spring term.

"By the end of that year, I was ready for a full-time job. However, there was no job waiting for me. The four-year schools—even the four-year school extension facilities—would not look at me because I did not have a Ph.D. The public schools did not want me either. One personnel officer in one of the public school systems told me candidly that budgets were tight in the major area systems. The systems would be reluctant to hire someone with a master's degree and teaching experience when they could hire a beginning teacher for less money.

"Then, perhaps two weeks before the beginning of the fall semester, I got a call from the division chairman who had supervised me at one of the NVCC campuses. An English teacher had just resigned. Would I like to teach full-time?

"And so I was hired. The hiring process was different in 1970 than it is today. Were a teacher to resign close to the beginning of a school term today, that teacher's classes would be assigned to adjunct faculty while the hiring procedure was put into place. The position would be advertised; a selection committee would be assembled; and, with a bit of luck, a new teacher would be chosen three months later, ready to assume duties at the beginning of the next term. That is, the hiring procedure would be put into place if, indeed, we were allowed to retain the vacated position. Sometimes vacated positions rise in a kind of mist and disappear, only to be rained down upon some dryer area of the college."

WHAT THE WORK IS LIKE

"Full-time English faculty generally teach fifteen hours a week. For most of us, that is five three-hour classes. All of us teach at least some composition classes. In addition we may teach literature classes, technical writing, writing for business, creative writing, or other special electives approved by the State of Virginia for teaching at the freshman or sophomore level.

"I teach fifteen hours a week. I also have ten office hours a week, five of which follow a fixed schedule and five of which are 'flexible.' By my choice, all my classes are in the morning. I'm on campus five days a week by about 7:45—my first class begins at 8:00—and I leave campus every day by about 12:30. (I have colleagues who prefer an afternoon or evening schedule; I have other colleagues who like to squeeze all their teaching into four days a week.)

"In addition, I return to campus some afternoons for meetings or workshops or special projects. Still, most of my working time is spent off campus, preparing for my classes or grading papers. In fact, sometimes it feels as if *all* I do is grade papers.

"Sometime early in my teaching career at the college—perhaps during my third year—I kept track for several months of the time I was spending on my job—teaching, keeping office hours, attending meetings, preparing for classes, and grading papers. I found I was spending, on the average, seventy hours a week. I spend less now, of course, but I still do not have a forty-hour-per-week job."

THE UPSIDES

"I like the people—the students, my colleagues. It is fortunate that I do. Unlike the other campuses of the college—and unlike most other colleges—our campus is constructed without individual faculty offices. We have, instead, large office areas in which individual 'office space'—containing a desk, a bookcase or two, and a file cabinet—is defined by five-foot-high dividers. The humanities division office houses about forty people—faculty, three secretaries, a division chair. We share about twenty-five wastebaskets and four telephone lines. We have no privacy, but we're never lonely.

"I like the potential to 'do good.' True, I don't approach my work with quite the idealistic fervor I did, say, thirty years ago, but I still believe in what I am doing. I still believe that I can help students think more critically and communicate more effectively and that if the wind is blowing in the right direction I may even be able to excite some of them about literature.

"I like the schedule flexibility of college teaching. I like the fact that, within limits, I can determine the hours of the day and the days of the week when I will be teaching. I might not have as much freedom if I were on a smaller campus or if my department comprised a group all coveting the same schedule."

THE DOWNSIDES

"What I like least about my work is the grading. Grading is different from marking, and marking is certainly the most tedious part of my work. But marking, as tiring as it is, is, at least ideally, of profit to the students. They learn something from the marks and comments on the papers, if they give those marks any attention at all.

"But grading—evaluating whether work is competent (that is whether it merits a C), whether its quality exceeds what the average competent student produces (and, hence, merits a B or an A), or whether it is less than competent, average, college-level work (D or F)—putting that mark on the paper and, worse, assigning a grade for the semester are stress-producing exercises.

"Many students today equate C with failure; also, many think of a grade as a fairly arbitrary measure that can be adjusted through proper and persistent negotiation. Students have told me they 'need a B'; otherwise, they will lose their scholarship, their student visa, their chance to transfer, their permission to continue to attend college, their family's respect. And some of what they tell me is probably true. I do not like hurting a student's feelings. When a student has put forth extraordinary effort during an academic term but has produced less-than-competent work, I have wished I could reward intentions. Of course, I cannot."

SALARIES

"Our college is advertising positions (not in English) with a posted (nine-month) salary range of $31,736 to $50,635. The lower figure would be for an instructor; the higher for an associate professor.

"Starting rank is determined by education and experience. Someone with fifteen graduate hours beyond the master's degree in the teaching field and with six years' teaching experience would be hired as an assistant professor; someone with a master's degree and no experience would be hired as an instructor. In fact, though, a person with no teaching experience would not very likely be hired at all.

"Once faculty are hired, their salary grows by across-the-board cost-of-living increases determined annually by the General Assembly or by the increase that comes with promotion. Those faculty members who have been at the college for twenty-five to thirty years like I have been, and who are professors or associate professors, earn a nine-month salary of about $50,000 to $55,000.

"Summer teaching salaries are their own special animal. A faculty member may teach a specified number of hours (six, perhaps; the formula varies from year to year) at a salary proportional to his or her annual salary; hours beyond that are paid at some other—lower—rate.

"Of course, summer teaching is voluntary. Some faculty choose not to teach in the summer; others seek a full load."

ADVICE FROM ELLEN RAPHAELI

"A person who wants to teach at the community college level in the greater Washington area will do well to major in something other than English, or, if one's academic heart is in seventeenth century literature, to have an additional, more marketable, specialization—establishing distance learning or teaching the learning disabled or teaching English as a second language, for example. The community college population is growing, but traditional English departments are not. My department has actually shrunk by twenty percent over the last six to eight years. We have not suffered reductions in faculty (RIFs), but when English faculty have left the college, their faculty slots have been reassigned to other departments whose need has been greater than ours. Our last three or four positions were given to English as a Second Language (a separate department within our academic division).

"A person seeking a community college teaching position should be very technology savvy—less a problem for a young person than for an old-timer like me.

"There are strong social dimensions to teaching, and I think one has really to like other people and to be marginally comfortable with oneself to be happy in the work. A teacher has to be able to talk to an angry student, for example, without becoming personally angry or defensive.

"Having a sense of humor is helpful, too. It is good to be able to laugh with a class, to lighten things up a bit when material is heavy, and it is good to be able to laugh at yourself rather than being absolutely mortified when you say or do something really foolish in front of twenty-five people from whom you wish respect. Finally, it's probably good not to say or do really foolish things very often."

Rosemary Day—English Instructor

Rosemary Day is an English instructor at Albuquerque TVI Community College, a community college/voc-tech institute in New Mexico. She earned her B.A. in English and her M.A. in humanities at State University of New York (SUNY) at Buffalo, and her Ph.D. in English at the University of New Mexico. She has been teaching since 1979.

GETTING STARTED

"This will sound sentimental, but I have always wanted to be a teacher, since childhood, when I taught my dolls. Every level of learning I progressed through, my goals changed—from teaching kindergarten to fifth grade to junior high to senior high—until in college I realized I wanted to have adult interaction with the people I taught.

"Also, I have lived a vicarious life through good literature, and that started in childhood, as well. There was little likelihood I would have majored in anything but literature and English. When I returned to school for my doctorate, my main motivation was the need to communicate with people in a learning environment about the material I was reading; to read in isolation left me desiring connection. Teaching English fulfills all that, the love for written material and the need for human connection.

"I got my first job when I was living in a small town in Northern New Mexico. I put in a resume at a university extension center and was hired on the spot. I taught three college courses in the evening at the high school that first semester. I taught there part-time for three years and then went back to school for my doctorate.

"For my current job, I had my resume and application in at the community college and all area secondary schools, public and private. I taught two courses a semester at the university and was hired part-time at the voc-tech community college. I was interviewed for a full-time position the following summer and was hired."

WHAT THE WORK IS LIKE

"My students are varied: seventeen to sixties, single, married, many with children, liberal arts college freshman and sophomores, and vocational-tech students in a range of programs—computer programming and networking, accounting and business, design drafting tech, health occupations, electronics engineering tech, culinary arts, legal assistance. They are culturally varied, too— Anglo, Hispanic, Native American, Asian, African-American.

"I teach several courses. English 101, first semester college composition, is required in both liberal arts and voc-tech programs. English 102, second semester composition (analytic writing), is required in a few programs, but most of the students plan to transfer to colleges and universities where it is required and take it at TVI while completing their first two years. This can be an elective in some of the associate's degree programs.

"English 119, technical communication, is a requirement for many voc-tech programs and is always filled to capacity. It has an interesting and dynamic mix of students. English 240, traditional grammar, is required by some business programs and students majoring in education; some of the students simply take it because they want to.

"English 296, American literature, fulfills a literature requirement for education majors; it also draws students just as an elective to meet English and humanities credits.

"Fall and spring semesters I teach six courses and the summer semester I teach three, for a total of fifteen courses (or forty-five credit hours) a year. The salary level where I work and the need for year-round benefit coverage require that I teach this load. I overload in fall and spring so that my part-time summer load is lighter; it ranges thirty to forty-five hours a week (usually forty); fall and spring workweeks range fifty to seventy-five hours.

"I meet with students in eighteen hours of class time and six office hours, plus I put in six official 'duty hours.' On paper, it looks like a thirty-hour week, but add preparation and grading eighty to one hundred essays, plus technical communication assignments, and there are at least another twenty hours a week.

"Then there are meetings—departmental, discipline, and those relevant to other activities. For example, I am involved with distance education, teaching a course on the Internet, committees, and satellite televised conferences.

"Summers I teach twelve weeks: four hours per class or twelve class hours, office hours, duty hours, and then grading and preparation. I often do further preparation for fall over the summer, especially because I am redesigning a course for delivery on the Internet that I teach in the fall.

"A typical day? I run into former and current students in hallways and talk and find out how they are doing. My classes are quite active; I move around the room, trying to create interaction and discussion, helping students work in groups or individually. I sit only for brief times on desks or tabletops. I love the way the world drops away while I am in class; nothing else seems to exist. I am totally in the moment, which I find quite fulfilling. I often barely manage to eat or take a break on my long days, usually two a week. I visit with faculty in all disciplines in hallways, in my or their offices, by the microwave or the copy machine. That helps all of us stay current and not isolated in our disciplines. I really do like how full these days are, even though they are tiring.

"The two shorter days I have I teach one or two classes and grade and prep. Fridays we often have meetings since those days have been left open for that purpose."

THE UPSIDES

"I think what I like most is being so totally in the moment when I am teaching and the fulfillment that comes with seeing students learning to believe in themselves; that transformation in a student is wonderful to see. The thank you's are nice, but seeing the change is thank you enough for me. At a community college, we get some students who are unsure of their ability to do college work; when they learn they can do it, that self-belief furthers their ability to do well."

THE DOWNSIDES

"The downside of teaching five composition courses a semester plus usually a technical communications course is that I spend half of all my weekends grading (usually every other weekend.) Last fall, however, I did not have a day off after Labor Day until Thanksgiving. Teaching the on-line course was one factor because on-line discussion rooms and e-mail interaction with students took the time of two to three classes. However, I do find distance education exciting. It is an area of professional growth and learning for me as much as it is for the students."

SALARIES

"My salary is about $29,200 to $29,500 for two semesters— I've been there ten years. I teach three semesters a year to make $42,000 to $44,000, before taxes, of course."

ADVICE FROM ROSEMARY DAY

"Get an M.A. or Ph.D. in English. Jobs are tight, so be prepared to teach part-time for a long time. Try to keep other options open, such as editing and technical writing.

"You may be required to take some courses in education, but the most valuable how-to-teach learning occurs while you're actually teaching.

"Keep your resume uncluttered and your cover letter to one page. I have sat in on the review process, and long wordy accounts of your great academic prowess is not seen as relevant to the needs of voc-tech junior college students.

"Of course, be sure your resume and letter are meticulously accurate. They serve as examples of your own care and intelligence and as models of what you will teach and require of students in a tech comm course.

"Once hired, be open to feedback from students and ideas from other teachers. Stay open and fluid. Texts, approaches, and technology are all changing for us and our students and in the work world our students enter. They need to learn adaptability as well.

"Don't be afraid of technology, computers, Word, Excel, Powerpoint (great for classroom presentations—and it gives the teacher control of the material), and the Internet. Students need guidance in using these wisely, for example, evaluating the credibility of a website when conducting research."

Joy Davis—Basic Skills Instructor

Joy Davis is an instructor at Bessemer State Technical College a community/technical college in Bessemer, Alabama. She started her work in this field in 1977.

In 1974 she earned her B.A. in English from the University of Montevallo in Alabama and, ten years later, her M.A. in higher education from the University of Alabama in Tuscaloosa.

GETTING STARTED

"As a child, I would pretend to teach my stuffed animals. Teaching seemed a natural field for me.

"I taught English and Spanish in a private academy as my first job. This gave me teaching experience. But, I trained for adult education on the job. Teaching adults is something I had to learn by doing.

"Luckily, when I graduated from college, there was an immediate opening in a small private school near my home. I was offered the job and took it.

"But teaching high school wasn't fulfilling for me. I was close in age to many of the seniors in my class. Fortunately, a friend of mine was president of the community college in my town. There was an opening in the ABE center in the college. I applied and got the job."

WHAT THE WORK IS LIKE

"All students who come to Bessemer State are required to take the ASSET placement test. Each major area of study sets its own set of criteria for placement scores. If students do not meet the designated score for the chosen major, then they are enrolled in developmental courses to try to improve their skills. For example, the designated reading score for a major area such as accounting might be 42. If a student scores below 42 on the ASSET test, that student is enrolled in the basic reading course to try to improve reading skills. When skills improve, he or she then goes into the required classes to complete the requirements for the degree. Bad news: if the skills don't improve (students are allowed three semesters of remediation), the student cannot move forward. The same holds true for English and math. So, I teach students from all majors.

"Sometimes, a student may feel he or she needs a brushup on reading or English. We have many students who return to school after many years on a job. (Our average student age is thirty-three). Sometimes, these students feel they aren't ready for the required courses, so they enroll themselves in the developmental courses first.

"Along with the basic skills courses—basic reading and English skills—I also teach voc-tech English to our college students who want a certificate or diploma in a certain program such as welding, automotive, and nursing. Alabama state law requires that all students who complete a program in a community college have basic English and math courses. So, I teach everything from basic reading to advanced English composition.

"Teachers in the college system in Alabama are required to work forty hours a week. Also, we must post our office hours for student conferences. On a typical day, I report at 7:30 A.M. On most mornings, I have an 8:00 class. Usually, the 8:00 hour is set aside for developmental courses, such as basic writing.

"Developmental courses are counted as noncredit toward a degree. However, students are given institutional credit. (Developmental courses used to be called remedial courses, but the term remedial is no longer used.) One advantage to these brush-up courses is that students receive grades of S (satisfactory) or IP (in progress). These grades cannot impact their overall GPA scores. So a student is never penalized for taking developmental courses.

"The whole purpose of developmental courses is that they allow students to acquire the skills they need without fear of failing. Also, taking developmental course work entitles students to free tutoring services, mentoring, and, in some cases, additional financial aid. So even though they don't receive a regular grade, they do have some perks. The only bad thing about the developmental courses is that they are not at this time transferable to other institutions.

"During the day, I teach three to four classes, grade endless stacks of compositions, and try to be available for conferences. When classes are over, I must prepare for the next day's classes. I have to make sure I have the proper handouts, that I have papers graded promptly, and that I know the material.

"Usually, the days are fairly hectic. There are always students who need to see me, always papers to grade, and always additional paperwork to be completed. Since we are federally funded, we must keep accurate rolls. We call roll every class meeting, drop students who miss a certain number of days, refer students for personal counseling...and then we must keep up with all of that paperwork."

THE UPSIDES

"One of the wonderful things about teaching at the college is the working environment. I have some very good friends who work with me. Since I've been at the college for so long, I know just about everyone. I do have time during most days to chat with co-workers.

"The most rewarding part of my job is something that all teachers anticipate. It is the student who, almost in an instant, expresses understanding. When I am lecturing, I look at my students. I watch their expressions, hoping that I will see that one look that says, 'Oh, yes, I understand now.' When I see it, I breathe a sigh of relief.

"Many times, when I'm ready to give up, it's that look that keeps me going. So, more than anything else, the students keep me wanting to teach.

"Occasionally, a student will come back after finishing a class and tell me that he or she is grateful for the stringent demands I impose on my students. I expect a great deal from my students, but I think I give a great deal in return. And I tell them that at the beginning of each semester. I expect their best in return for mine.

"Many of our students have gone on to four-year colleges, many have found wonderful jobs, and many have won high honors in different areas. They come to us usually afraid that they cannot succeed. Oftentimes, our students have failed at other attempts at school. Some have lost their jobs, most have families to support, and most are intimidated by the college environment, in addition to being beset with personal problems. Most of our students work full-time or part-time, so studying is difficult.

"The best part of my job is convincing the students that they can succeed. If I can convince even a few that learning is possible, that achieving academic goals is fulfilling, then I've done a good day's work. Quite a few of our students have started in developmental courses, finished them successfully, gone on to the required course work, and then achieved academic degrees with honors.

"We have a graduation ceremony once a year. Watching these students walk across that stage and seeing the looks on their faces and the support and pride of their families is absolutely amazing."

THE DOWNSIDES

"The worst part of my job is the grading. Our grading system is comparable to that of a four-year college. Our standards are fairly high. Sometimes, no matter how hard I try, I cannot seem to help a student. When a student fails, I feel bad, especially when the student has worked hard.

"Another not-so-likable part of the job is the endless stream of paperwork, forms for virtually everything."

SALARIES

"Salaries for teachers are set by rank, with rank IV being the highest, rank I the lowest. Teachers in community/technical colleges are ranked according to degree and experience. The entry-level positions now require a master's degree in-field and some years of teaching experience.

"Beginning teachers earn approximately $30,000, while those in higher ranks earn $45,000 to $60,000."

ADVICE FROM JOY DAVIS

"Teaching, at its easiest, is difficult. Teaching adults is even harder. Many of them must 'unlearn' things they've been doing for years. To enjoy teaching, a person must be patient, compassionate, and willing to struggle to show students how a certain task is done correctly.

"Teaching is emotionally draining and physically demanding, but well worth the effort. Getting a master's degree now is essential for anyone who wants to teach. Of course, the higher the degree, the better the chance of obtaining employment. Prospective teachers should begin by teaching some part-time courses at local community or technical colleges. Teaching just one course can give a person experience in being in command of a classroom full of adult learners. Tutoring and mentoring can also be vehicles for teaching experience.

"Teaching is certainly not for everyone. You won't get rich, but you will have enriching experiences."

Geraldine Mosher—Computer Instructor

Geraldine Mosher is a computer instructor with Albuquerque Technical-Vocational Institute in New Mexico. She started her work there in 1984 as a math and English tutor in the Adult Learning Center. She began as a computer instructor with their Continuing Education Division a year and a half later, then moved recently to their Workforce Training Center.

She earned her B.A. from the University of Michigan, Ann Arbor, with a major in English and minors in chemistry and Spanish in 1962. She earned her M.A. in education from Century University in Albuquerque, New Mexico, with a specialization in adult education in 1992.

In addition, she took the following computer programming and training courses from Albuquerque TVI from 1983 to 1995: Intro to Data Processing, Basic Language Programming (Beginning and Advanced), Pascal Programming, ANSI Cobol Programming (Beginning and Advanced), DBase III Programming, C Language Programming (Beginning and Advanced), Fortran Programming, Intro to Microcomputing, Advanced Lotus 1–2-3, Intro to the UNIX Operating System, Creating Documents with PageMaker, Basic Internet.

GETTING STARTED

"I always knew that I had the ability to teach. However, I was disappointed with the discipline problems in the public school system and, therefore, did not go into the field of teaching. It was not until I finished with my other career (twenty years with the Foreign Service at embassies and consulates overseas) that I realized that by teaching adults I would usually not have to cope with people who didn't want to learn.

"When I was in college to get my B.A., I took all of the required education courses to obtain my teacher's certificate; I lacked only one semester of student teaching in order to qualify. I did not ever get my teacher's certificate, however, because I decided not to go into teaching at that time. Later, I got my knowledge of computers from many continuing education courses and received my master's degree in adult education.

"For my first job in this field, I applied to be an English and math tutor at Albuquerque Technical-Vocational Institute (TVI) and passed both tests and the interview. While I was working at TVI, a memo was circulated to all offices, asking everyone if they were interested in teaching any continuing education classes. I responded that I was qualified to teach computer classes, and I was hired.

"I worked for TVI's Continuing Education Division for approximately eleven years. I taught various computer classes including Computer Literacy, DOS, Quicken, Windows, and WordPerfect. Then TVI discontinued the Continuing Education Division, and all duties were assumed by either the Workforce Training Center (training for businesses) or the Emeritus Classes (training for senior citizens).

"My present position with Albuquerque TVI is with the Workforce Training Center. I still teach basically the same subjects: Introduction to Computers, Windows, Quicken, and WordPerfect."

WHAT THE WORK IS LIKE

"Teaching adults through the Continuing Education Division or the Workforce Training Center of Albuquerque Technical-Vocational Institute is a relatively easy and rewarding way to teach. First of all, you teach only subjects you agree to teach because you feel comfortable teaching those subjects. Secondly, you have a relatively free reign as to how you teach, as long as the appropriate subject matter is covered in the allotted time.

"The continuing education classes were usually twelve hours in length (beginning or intermediate Windows, for example). Those twelve hours would be broken up into two Saturdays of six hours each (three in the morning and three in the afternoon). If you taught them during the week, the twelve hours would be broken up into three sessions of four hours each on different days, for example, three consecutive Monday afternoons.

"Continuing education classes included both people who were sent by their employer to take the classes, and private individuals who just wanted to learn something and paid for the classes themselves.

"The training sessions taught through the Workforce Training Center might be a one-time full-day class (six to seven hours) or might be two-hour classes once a week for six to eight weeks. The Workforce Training Center contracts with businesses to train their employees. Therefore, the students are not totally volunteers—raises or promotions may depend on their taking the classes.

"The classrooms are not always the greatest—sometimes too hot or cold, sometimes very crowded quarters, sometimes the equipment is not working properly—but, all in all, a most pleasant working experience."

THE UPSIDES

"The greatest reward about teaching is the thrill when 'the light bulb goes on,'—that is, when a student has struggled with some concept or exercise and then finally all is clear and he or she understands what you have been teaching."

THE DOWNSIDES

"The part I dislike the most is the administrative details—checking that the people attending match the names on the roster and also having the students fill out evaluation forms after every class."

SALARIES

"The salary for both the Continuing Education Division and the Workforce Training Center was either $22 or $32 per hour of teaching (no pay for any preparation work), depending on what you taught.

"The greatest drawback is that you are not assured of a certain minimum number of hours. The schedule for continuing education classes was set up a semester at a time. However, if enough students did not enroll for a particular class, the class was canceled, and you would receive no compensation.

"Teaching for the Workforce Training Center is even more haphazard. When a company contacts TVI to arrange for computer training in a particular subject—Excel, for example—the Workforce Training Center contacts an instructor who is qualified to teach that subject. The instructor can then accept or refuse the assignment."

ADVICE FROM GERALDINE MOSHER

"To teach in an adult education situation requires excellent knowledge of the subject matter, more than any particular degree. Be willing to start at a low salary to prove yourself, and be willing to go beyond the requirements of the job.

"A good way to learn the ropes is to sit in on other teachers' classes so you can observe what works and what doesn't, what you like and what you don't.

"Most important, I believe that anyone who enters the teaching profession, whether teaching adults or children, should love to teach beyond all else."

CHAPTER 5

CAREER AND VOCATIONAL COUNSELING

Career and vocational counselors assist individuals in making and implementing informed educational and occupational choices. They help students or clients to develop competencies in self-knowledge, educational and occupational exploration, and career planning.

Career and vocational counseling is an integral part of adult education and key to its effective delivery. Good counseling programs help individuals acquire the knowledge, skills, and experience necessary to identify options, explore alternatives, and succeed in society. These programs better prepare individuals for the changing workplace by teaching labor market changes and complexity of the workplace, improving decision-making skills, increasing self-esteem and motivation, building interpersonal effectiveness, maximizing career opportunities, improving employment marketability and opportunities, promoting effective job placement, and strengthening employer relations.

THE DIFFERENT TYPES OF COUNSELORS

High school counselors advise on college majors, admission requirements, entrance exams, and financial aid, and on trade, technical school, and apprenticeship programs. They help students develop job finding skills such as resume writing and interviewing techniques.

College career planning and placement counselors assist alumni or students with career development and job hunting techniques.

Elementary school counselors observe younger children during classroom and play activities and confer with their teachers and parents to evaluate their strengths, problems, or special needs. They also help students develop good study habits. They do less vocational and academic counseling than secondary school counselors.

School counselors at all levels help students understand and deal with their social, behavioral, and personal problems. They emphasize preventive and developmental counseling to provide students with the life skills needed to deal with problems before they occur, and to enhance personal, social, and academic growth.

School counselors work with students individually, in small groups, or with entire classes. They consult and work with parents, teachers, school administrators, school psychologists, school nurses, and social workers.

Rehabilitation counselors help people deal with the personal, social, and vocational effects of their disabilities. They may counsel people with disabilities resulting from birth defects, illness or disease, accidents, or the stress of daily life. They evaluate the strengths and limitations of individuals, provide personal and vocational counseling, and may arrange for medical care, vocational training, and job placement.

Rehabilitation counselors interview individuals with disabilities and their families, evaluate school and medical reports, and confer and plan with physicians, psychologists, occupational therapists, and employers to determine the capabilities and skills of the individual. Conferring with the client, they develop a rehabilitation program, which may include training to help the person develop job skills. They also work toward increasing the client's capacity to live independently.

Career and employment counselors help individuals make wise career decisions. They explore and evaluate the client's education, training, work history, interests, skills, and personal traits, and may arrange for aptitude and achievement tests. They also work with individuals to develop job seeking skills and assist clients in locating and applying for jobs.

Mental health counselors emphasize prevention and work with individuals and groups to promote optimum mental health. They help individuals deal with addictions and substance abuse, suicide, stress management, problems with self-esteem, issues associated with aging, job and career concerns, educational decisions, issues of mental and emotional health, and family, parenting, and marital problems. Mental health counselors work closely with other mental health specialists, including psychiatrists, psychologists, clinical social workers, psychiatric nurses, and school counselors.

Other counseling specialties include marriage and family, multicultural, or gerontological counseling.

- A *gerontological counselor* provides services to elderly persons who face changing lifestyles due to health problems and helps families cope with these changes.
- A *multicultural counselor* helps employers adjust to an increasingly diverse workforce.

Counselors provide special services, including alcohol and drug prevention programs and classes that teach students to handle conflicts without resorting to violence. Counselors also try to identify cases involving domestic abuse and other family problems that can affect a student's development.

Counselors use interviews, counseling sessions, tests, or other methods when evaluating and advising students. They may operate career information centers and career education programs.

KEY COMPONENTS OF SUCCESSFUL COUNSELING PROGRAMS

The following have been identified by the U.S. Department of Education, Office of Vocational and Adult Education, as key components in successful career guidance and counseling programs:

- A planned sequence of activities and experiences to achieve specific competencies such as self-appraisal, decision making, goal setting, and career planning
- Accountability (outcome oriented) and program improvement (based on results of process/outcome evaluations)
- Qualified leadership
- Effective management needed to support comprehensive career guidance programs
- A team approach in which certified counselors are central to the program
- Adequate facilities, materials, and resources
- Strong professional development activities so counselors can regularly update their professional knowledge and skills
- Different approaches to deliver the program such as outreach, assessment, counseling, curriculum, program and job placement, follow-up, consultation, referral

PARTICIPANTS AND SETTINGS

Anyone can benefit from career and vocational counseling. Career exploration can begin with young students in the primary grades and continue through the secondary years. Career counselors also work with adults—male and female—disabled, disadvantaged, minorities, non-native English speakers, the incarcerated, school dropouts, single parents, displaced homemakers, teachers, administrators, parents, and employers.

Vocational and educational counselors hold about 175,000 jobs nationwide. Counseling programs are offered almost everywhere: elementary, junior, and senior high schools; community colleges; technical institutes; universities and career resource centers; correctional facilities; human services agencies; health care facilities; community and business organizations; skill clinics and employment and placement service centers; job training, career development, and vocational rehabilitation centers; social agencies; and residential care facilities such as halfway houses for criminal offenders and group homes for children, the aged, and the disabled.

Counselors also work in organizations engaged in community improvement and social change, as well as drug and alcohol rehabilitation programs and state and local government agencies.

A growing number of counselors work in health maintenance organizations, insurance companies, group practice, and private practice. This growth has been spurred by laws allowing counselors to receive payments from insurance companies and requiring employers to provide rehabilitation and counseling services to employees.

OPPORTUNITIES FOR CAREER
AND VOCATIONAL COUNSELORS

Through a variety of adult education programs and settings, counselors have many opportunities to participate in an education and training system that integrates academic and vocational education, that encourages individuals' participation in further education, that allows counselors to renew their commitment to serving the most at-risk or disadvantaged of our society, and to respond to business and economic development.

Counseling services are offered to adult students in a variety of programs such as ABE and GED prep programs, in welfare-to-work programs and school-to-work programs, and in all the settings mentioned earlier in this chapter.

Here is just one example of an effective education program that utilizes career counselors to the fullest:

School-to-Work Opportunities

The School-to-Work Opportunities Act, signed by President Clinton on May 4, 1994, provides federal funds—seed capital—to the states to create comprehensive, coherent, statewide school-to-work opportunities systems that prepare all individuals for high wage, high skill jobs in a competitive global marketplace. These systems contain three core elements: school-based learning, work-based learning, and connecting activities.

"Graduates of these systems receive a high school diploma or its equivalent in addition to a recognized skills certificate. Others receive a certificate or diploma indicating completion of one or two years of postsecondary education, while others enter a registered apprenticeship program or enroll in a college or university. The act emphasizes the importance of counselors in building successful school-to-work systems.

School-to-work opportunities are an exciting and dynamic new way of learning geared toward preparing all youth for career employment, further education, and lifelong learning. Individuals are prepared for first jobs in high skill, high wage careers, achieve high academic and occupational standards, and are prepared for further postsecondary education and training.

School-to-Work Counselors

For career guidance and counseling to be effective, all counselors, not just career counselors, must become proactive in their efforts to assist students and adults maximize their career opportunities. All counselors must:

- Help individuals acquire the knowledge, skill, and experience necessary to discover their interests, identify career clusters and options, get a clear picture of the changing nature of work and careers, explore alternatives, make choices, and succeed in society
- Work together with teachers, other school staff, students, parents, employers, and the broader community to influence the learning and career development of individuals
- Help individuals make the connection between what they are learning and the broad range of career possibilities
- Form broad-based partnerships with all of those involved in helping individuals join the worlds of school and work
- Assist individuals master workplace basics
- Help individuals find appropriate employment, continue their education and/or training, and find other community services necessary for a successful transition from school to work
- Coordinate individuals' career plans and portfolios to position them to reach their career goals

WORKING CONDITIONS

Most school counselors work the traditional nine- to ten-month school year with a two- to three-month vacation, although an increasing number are employed on ten-and-a-half- or eleven-month contracts. They generally have the same hours as teachers.

College career planning and placement counselors may work long and irregular hours during recruiting periods.

Rehabilitation and employment counselors generally work a standard forty-hour week.

Self-employed counselors and those working in mental health and community agencies often work evenings to counsel clients who work during the day.

Counselors must possess high physical and emotional energy to handle the array of problems they address. Dealing with these day-to-day problems can cause stress and emotional burnout.

Since privacy is essential for confidential and frank discussions with clients, counselors usually have private offices.

THE QUALIFICATIONS YOU'LL NEED

Recent data indicate that six out of ten counselors have a master's degree; fields of study include college student affairs, elementary or secondary school counseling, education, gerontological counseling, marriage and family counseling, substance abuse counseling, rehabilitation counseling, agency or community counseling, clinical mental health counseling, counseling psychology, career counseling, or a related field.

Graduate-level counselor education programs in colleges and universities usually are in departments of education or psychology. Courses are grouped into eight core areas:

human growth and development
social and cultural foundations
helping relationships
groups
lifestyle and career development
appraisal
research and evaluation
professional orientation

In an accredited program, forty-eight to sixty semester hours of graduate study, including a period of supervised clinical experience in counseling, are required for a master's degree.

More than one hundred institutions offer programs in counselor education, including career, community, gerontological, mental health, school, student affairs, and marriage and family counseling, accredited by the Council for Accreditation of Counseling and Related Educational Programs (CACREP).

In 1997 forty-two states and the District of Columbia had some form of counselor credentialing legislation, licensure, certification, or registry for practice outside schools. Requirements vary from state to state. In some states, credentialing is mandatory; in others, voluntary.

Many counselors elect to be nationally certified by the National Board for Certified Counselors (NBCC), which grants the general practice credential, National Certified Counselor. To be certified, a counselor must hold a master's degree in counseling from a regionally accredited institution, have at least two years of supervised professional counseling experience, and pass NBCC's National Counselor Examination for Licensure and Certification. This national certification is voluntary and distinct from state certification. However, in some states, those who pass the national exam are exempt from taking a state certification exam. NBCC also offers specialty certification in career, gerontological, school, clinical mental health, and addictions counseling.

To maintain their certification, counselors must complete one hundred hours of acceptable continuing education credit every five years.

All states require school counselors to hold state school counseling certification; however, certification requirements vary from state to state. Some states require public school counselors to have both counseling and teaching certificates.

Depending on the state, a master's degree in counseling and two to five years of teaching experience may be required for a counseling certificate.

Vocational and related rehabilitation agencies generally require a master's degree in rehabilitation counseling, counseling and guidance, or counseling psychology for rehabilitation counselor jobs. Some, however, may accept applicants with a bachelor's degree in rehabilitation services, counseling, psychology, sociology, or related fields.

A bachelor's degree may qualify a person to work as a counseling aide, rehabilitation aide, or social service worker. Experience in employment counseling, job development, psychology, education, or social work may be helpful.

The Council on Rehabilitation Education (CORE) accredits graduate programs in rehabilitation counseling. A minimum of two years of study—including six hundred hours of supervised clinical internship experience—are required for the master's degree.

In most state vocational rehabilitation agencies, applicants must pass a written examination and be evaluated by a board of examiners to obtain licensure. In addition, many employers require rehabilitation counselors to be nationally certified. To become certified by the Commission on Rehabilitation Counselor Certification, counselors must graduate from an accredited educational program, complete an internship, and pass a written examination. They are then designated as Certified Rehabilitation Counselors. To maintain their certification, counselors must complete one hundred hours of acceptable continuing education credit every five years.

Some states require counselors in public employment offices to have a master's degree; others accept a bachelor's degree with appropriate counseling courses.

Clinical mental health counselors generally have a master's degree in mental health counseling, another area of counseling, or in psychology or social work. They are voluntarily certified by the National Board for Certified Counselors. Generally, to receive certification as a clinical mental health counselor, a counselor must have a master's degree in counseling, two years of postmaster's experience, a period of supervised clinical experience, a taped sample of clinical work, and a passing grade on a written examination.

Some employers provide training for newly hired counselors. Many have work-study programs so that employed counselors can earn graduate degrees. Counselors must participate in graduate studies, workshops, institutes, and personal studies to maintain their certificates and licenses.

People interested in counseling should have a strong interest in helping others and the ability to inspire respect, trust, and confidence. They should be able to work independently or as part of a team.

Counselors follow the code of ethics associated with their respective certifications and licenses.

ADVANCEMENT OPPORTUNITIES

Prospects for advancement vary by counseling field. School counselors may move to a larger school; become directors or supervisors of counseling, guidance, or pupil personnel services; or, usually with further graduate education, become counselor educators, counseling psychologists, or school administrators.

Some counselors also may advance to work at the state department of education.

Rehabilitation, mental health, and employment counselors may become supervisors or administrators in their agencies. Some counselors move into research, consulting, or college teaching, or go into private or group practice.

JOB OUTLOOK

Overall employment of counselors is expected to grow about as fast as the average for all occupations through the year 2006. In addition, replacement needs should increase significantly as a large number of counselors reach retirement age.

Employment of school and vocational counselors is expected to grow as a result of increasing enrollments, particularly in secondary and postsecondary schools, state legislation requiring counselors in elementary schools, and the expanded responsibilities of counselors.

Counselors are becoming more involved in crisis and preventive counseling, helping students deal with issues ranging from drug and alcohol abuse to death and suicide. Also, the growing diversity of student populations is presenting challenges to counselors in dealing with multicultural issues.

Job growth among counselors, however, may be dampened by budgetary constraints. High student-to-counselor ratios in many schools could increase even more as student enrollments grow. When funding is tight, schools usually prefer to hire new teachers before adding counselors in an effort to keep classroom sizes at acceptable levels.

Rapid job growth is expected among rehabilitation and mental health counselors. Under managed care systems, insurance companies increasingly provide for reimbursement of counselors, enabling many counselors to move from schools and government agencies to private practice.

Counselors are also forming group practices to receive expanded insurance coverage. The number of people who need rehabilitation services will rise as advances in medical technology continue to save lives that only a few years ago would have been lost.

In addition, legislation requiring equal employment rights for people with disabilities will spur demand for counselors. Counselors not only will help individuals with disabilities with their transition into the workforce, but also will help companies comply with the law.

Employers are also increasingly offering employee assistance programs that provide mental health and alcohol and drug abuse services. A growing number of people are expected to use these services as the elderly population grows and as society focuses on ways of developing mental well-being, such as controlling stress associated with job and family responsibilities.

As with other government jobs, the number of employment counselors who work primarily for state and local government, could be limited by budgetary constraints. However, demand for government employment counseling may grow as new welfare laws require welfare recipients to find jobs.

Opportunities for employment counselors working in private job training services should grow as counselors provide skill training and other services to laid-off workers, experienced workers seeking a new or second career, full-time homemakers seeking to enter or reenter the workforce, and workers who want to upgrade their skills.

SALARIES

Median earnings for full-time educational and vocational counselors are about $35,800 a year. The middle 50 percent earns between $25,600 and $48,500 a year. The bottom 10 percent earns less than $18,600 a year, while the top 10 percent earns over $60,100 a year.

According to the Educational Research Service, the average salary of public school counselors in the 1995–96 academic year (the most recent figures available) was about $44,100. Many school counselors are compensated on the same pay scale as teachers. School counselors can earn additional income working summers in the school system or in other jobs.

Self-employed counselors who have well-established practices, as well as counselors employed in group practices, generally have the highest earnings, as do some counselors working for private firms, such as insurance companies, corporations, and private rehabilitation companies.

FIRSTHAND ACCOUNTS

The firsthand accounts that follow in this chapter include a career counselor, a social worker/student advocate, and a GED counselor/test administrator.

Adele Fuller—Career Counselor

Adele Fuller currently works as a freelance career counselor for The Phoenix Project, a welfare-to-work program sponsored by the City of Albuquerque. She also works as an adult educator with corporate clients for Albuquerque TVI, Workforce Training Division. In addition, she teaches writing seminars to small business owners through Southwest Writers Workshop and gives career facilitation skills workshops to agency personnel working with the welfare population through the New Mexico Career Development Association.

She earned her B.A. in English literature in 1966 from Gettysburg College in Pennsylvania and her M.A. in 1988 in counseling from Montclair University, Montclair, New Jersey.

GETTING STARTED

"Like many people, I fell into my profession after many years of uncertainty, wandering around and being a frustrated stay-at-home mom. It became apparent after years of volunteerism through church, children's schools, and community that I was drawn to groups—forming them, helping them grow, watching how they worked. Following this revelation of my interest in group dynamics, I returned to graduate school at the age of forty-one to get my M.A. in counseling, taking as many group dynamics courses as I could cram in. When I proudly got my degree at age forty-four, I still didn't have a clue as to what I would do with it. I knew I did not want to be a therapist and work with the mentally retarded, addicted, or developmentally handicapped populations. But what *did* I want to do?

"At that time my marriage deteriorated and ultimately ended in divorce. During those difficult years of personal despair and fear, it became clear who my population was. Women in transition! I went looking for a job at a community college that had some kind of outreach program for women and, after six long months of networking, found one. I was hired not only to run the Women's Outreach Program, but to help with unemployed men and women referred to us by JTPA (Job Training Partnership Act). Without quite realizing what was happening, I found myself becoming a career counselor.

"During my six years at the college, I counseled thousands of adults, both individually and through group seminars I designed and taught. It became apparent through these workshops that I not only needed good counseling skills, but good training/presentation skills as well, so I returned to the local community college and earned a

Train-the-Trainer certificate within a year's time. This gave me the added tools and confidence I needed to conceive, plan, design, and present a program to any population with professional competence. I found that my counseling skills, along with my newly honed presentation skills, put me in a position to teach not only career development issues, but other life issues, or 'soft skills,' as well.

"This led me to an interest in trying to gain corporate training experience outside my college employment, and over the next few years, I worked for outplacement agencies and put together customized training programs for local corporations in need of skills training for their employees. Topics might include: communication skills, assertiveness training, networking skills, career development, dealing with depression during the job search, etc.

"I also became a member of the Speaker's Bureau for the college and joined Toastmasters International to develop my speaking skills. Public speaking is a natural offshoot of training and group facilitation, I find, and can become a whole other way of educating an adult audience. While not essential to this field for those who are less extroverted, public speaking certainly enhances presentation skills and the ability to think on one's feet, which is what adult training is all about.

"After six years, I left my college position in New Jersey and relocated to Albuquerque, New Mexico. Since full-time jobs in my field are scarce here, I decided to see if I could survive as a freelancer. Though I moved here as a complete stranger, I found that my networking skills landed me fairly steady employment within a ten-month period. Career counselors get to practice what they teach, and now it is time for me to use all the tools I have brought to my many clients."

WHAT THE WORK IS LIKE

"At the present time I teach life-skills to welfare clients, communications and basic reading to corporate employees, and career facilitation skills to agency personnel who work with the welfare population. I am also helping to design and implement a writing course for small business owners so they may market their businesses more successfully.

"A typical day might look like this: 8:00 A.M. to 1:00 P.M. I present life-skills material to a current group of nine clients. Material will consist of discussion, written exercises, activities, and feedback sessions. After class, I may have a one-hour session with a member of the class. Then a short fifteen-minute check-in with other instructors and staff members to communicate about background issues; teamwork is essential in this environment. From 7:00 to 8:00 P.M., I spend preparing and reviewing my notes for the next day's class.

"Adult educators have two arenas in which they practice: the private arena, in which they design their curriculum, map out their lesson plans, and prepare, prepare, prepare for class; and the social arena, in which they perform as trainer/educator/entertainer. Because adults have a full suitcase of life experience, they are not taught like children. Rather, they are invited into an interactive dialogue in which their experience is affirmed just as new information is added. They must be respected, encouraged, and engaged as well as taught, and the patronizing or inept trainer will not be tolerated very long. Adults vote with their feet—they simply walk out.

"Most trainers/educators enjoy the delivery more than the planning but soon learn that thorough planning is essential to a good delivery, so equal energy must be given to both. A trainer is often like a writer or an entertainer in that he or she is always collecting anecdotes, toys, and gimmicks to use as educational devices in the classroom. The best trainers have a spontaneous, down-to-earth style; an excellent sense of humor; and an ability to roll with the punches that their group delivers. Like most other things in life, this takes lots of practice.

"As a freelancer, I typically spend about ten to fifteen hours a week in the classroom actually training. Another five hours will go toward preparation time, along with five to ten hours for background meetings, networking with potential clients, phone calls, and woolgathering for new ideas and materials. No two days are alike, and I have great flexibility with my time as I'm not in a nine-to-five job. This is highly enjoyable for a personality who likes change, freedom, independence, and creativity."

THE UPSIDES

"Advantages include working with a highly diverse population of all economic, ethnic, and educational levels, as well as coming into contact with people from all over—whether local or national, depending upon the scope of your practice. I also love the interaction with my students; I am always learning as much as I am teaching. People share their lives, their dreams, their struggles as we move through the material together, and it is extremely rewarding to observe adults not only absorb the material but make substantial changes and improvements in their lives as well. This is the feedback and the reward that goes beyond any paycheck. At the end of the day I feel my work has mattered, and that makes everything else bearable."

THE DOWNSIDES

"On the downside, as a freelancer, work can be unpredictable, income often unsteady, and I am responsible for carrying my own health insurance and retirement plan. Freedom vs. security is a daily reality. For those who find this uncomfortable, finding a steady job within an academic or corporate environment is another alternative. However, please be aware you'll be doing much more than training/educating in most cases. There are always administrative duties and other tasks that will inevitably comprise part of the job description."

SALARIES

"In an academic institution, such as a community college, starting salaries might range from $22,000 to $25,000 a year. In-house corporate trainers are usually part of the human resources department and paid a professional salary because they do other things as well.

"Freelance trainers might be paid anywhere from $18 to $35 an hour, depending on the job, the client, and the geographic area. Much higher salaries are earned by trainers who become involved in organizational development, a field demanding either more education or corporate experience or both. (I have a friend who never works for less than $400 a day, which is considered average for her level of competence.)

"Obviously, research into your local area is required here, as there are many different ways adult educators are employed."

ADVICE FROM ADELE FULLER

"If you find you love working in a group adult environment, enjoy motivating others toward knowledge and full living, and don't mind being in front of people, facilitating the learning experience, then adult education/training might be for you.

"Whether you enter through the door of career counseling, as I did, or as an Adult Basic Education (ABE) teacher, certain fundamental themes emerge: a passion for learning as well as teaching, an ability to communicate orally, an interest in preparing and/or designing class materials, and a humility that accompanies every experience in front of an audience.

"Adult educators must be part motivational personalities, part teachers, part clowns, and totally passionate about their work to be truly effective. The learning curve never stops, but neither do the rewards.

"Formal education to get you started could include writing, presentation, and counseling/training skills. Anything to do with human communication—from literature to psychology—is helpful, along with specific programs in counseling, education, and/or adult training. If you are teaching a technical subject, such as computers or mechanical skills, obviously expertise is needed in that field.

"An M.A. in a related field, whether counseling, education, or business, is certainly helpful but not always necessary in certain areas. Additional activities that would help are studying public speaking skills, participating in and learning about group dynamics, improving writing skills, and networking diligently to find out what training subjects are needed in your community. People with extroverted personalities, an ability to communicate, a need for daily variety in the workplace, and a strong desire to help others may thrive in this field."

Cheryl-Lani Branson—Social Worker/Student Advocate

Cheryl-Lani Branson was a social worker/student advocate in BEGIN, a welfare-to-work adult education program through Brooklyn College in Brooklyn, New York, from 1996 to 1997. She earned her B.A. in English literature in 1975 from the University of Hartford in Connecticut, her M.A. in counselor education from Queens College of the City University of New York in 1980, and in 1994 her master's in social work (M.S.W.) from Hunter College School of Social Work in New York City.

GETTING STARTED

"I went back to social work school to become an EAP counselor (employee assistance), but when I got out of school, every single company doing EAP was downsizing, as were most social work departments. Counseling the unemployed is not that different from counseling the employed, so it was a natural transition from trying to find work in EAP to becoming a counselor in a welfare-to-work adult education program.

"I got a master's degree in counseling many years ago and had interned at both a college and a vocational rehabilitation facility. When I returned to school for my master's in social work, I interned with both displaced homemakers and at a psychiatric facility. These internships trained me in a broad range of skills I could use with any client population. Additionally, I trained in group work while obtaining my master's in social work, which strengthened my abilities to teach coping skills to the adult education population.

"For this job, I responded to an ad in the *New York Times;* I did not get the job originally. The person they chose walked off the job the second day. I was called back in and thought I had to sell myself again, but I already had the job. I was interviewed by five people to get this job."

WHAT THE WORK IS LIKE

"Students in this education-to-work program were mandated to attend by the Human Resources Department, the agency responsible for public assistance. The goal of the program was either to get them a job or educate them toward getting a GED—or both.

"The program was one week in class—adult basic education or a GED class—and one week at a work site. There were two alternating groups. The program was five months and students could be extended if they were close to getting their GED. Some clients did go on to college, but not many.

"I came to be a counselor in a program where there were a multitude of problems and no one to solve them for a very long time. The first thing I did was spend several weeks assessing the client population and staff needs; at the same time, I began counseling students in crisis right away.

"Within the first half hour of starting my job, I had a client who was suicidal. I also did some ongoing, longer-term counseling. For the most part, clients came on their own for counseling, but referrals also came from their adult ed teachers, from the public assistance staff, and the support staff.

"Often clients would come to see me after I had organized several workshops. Part of my job was locating speakers on a variety of topics that would educate the students, especially in the areas of health and mental health. For instance, I had speakers come to talk about domestic violence, which is a huge problem with this client population. After their talk, I had about eight clients come talk to me about their own domestic violence situations.

"I also did a workshop myself during student orientation called Coping with Change. Many of the students had spent years on public assistance, and coming into a full-time program was quite traumatic for them, so my workshop was an attempt to neutralize and normalize the stress they might be experiencing.

"Another piece of my work was advocacy. I worked at the Brooklyn College-BEGIN program before the welfare law changed, so part of the advocacy was in trying to get the clients to talk to legislators and make calls and register to vote so that maybe the public assistance laws wouldn't change. (Public assistance went from being an entitlement to being a work-for-benefit situation.)

"I was in a position to recommend policy, and more specifically, could recommend that a client be suspended from the program or be given an extension in order to work on their issues.

"Perhaps the largest bulk of my time was spent in assessment and referral of students (clients.) The vast majority of people who came to me needed a resource or referral. I referred clients to housing, legal, advocacy, health, learning disabilities, domestic violence, mental health, immigration, and substance abuse resources, to name a few.

"I arranged my days; I had a lot of freedom within the context of an eight-hour day. The work was never boring, and partially that's because, while some parts of the days had to be organized in advance, such as speakers, much of my day was following up with resources and making arrangements, talking with staff, looking at policy. This job had lots of opportunities for both networking and leading.

"Funny story about the work atmosphere: When I arrived on the job, a refrigerator was in the office I was put in. This was one of the reasons that my predecessor left after a day and a half. I had no problem with the refrigerator remaining, at least for a short time, as I felt it meant that staff would need to come in for their food, and that this would be a great way to get to know people. I was right; and I demonstrated my flexibility, as well."

THE UPSIDES

"I loved the ability to structure my day, to assess what need was the most important and follow up with it. I was part of a team in Student Services, and it was great to be part of a team.

"I very much enjoyed counseling the students, and had lots of fun working with the students to show them how to be advocates for themselves.

"Negotiating with resources was also enjoyable—negotiating with government employees to get clients exempt from the program to take care of difficulties (substance abuse, mental health issues), negotiating with Medicaid to get client services, negotiating with outside agencies to get speakers for the clients classes, and, in one case, negotiating with five different agencies to get a domestic violence victim the appropriate follow-up and care. That usually took a lot of follow-up, but once you utilized a resource well, you could count on it forever."

THE DOWNSIDES

"What I liked least about the job was the pay. With a master's in social work, I should have been making about $5,000 more than I did. This job, in the private sector, would have paid about $45,000 in the New York market."

SALARIES

"I started the job earning $31,000 and completed it at $32,000. The program was grant-funded, and so we had several months when we were not paid full salary because the money hadn't come in from the government. We were compensated at a later time. I was paid biweekly. Depending on the job market, one shouldn't earn less than $28,000 for this kind of work."

ADVICE FROM CHERYL-LANI BRANSON

"Minimally, one should have a master's degree in some kind of counseling to do this job, and preferably, a master's in social work.

"Specific training in case management and group work is a big help. Perhaps the best way to start, which is what I did, is to volunteer your time, see if you enjoy counseling, and then get formal training in counseling. Many organizations train their volunteers in specific techniques for working with clients.

"I think the qualities you should possess to make you successful with this kind of work are the abilities to multitask, good follow through, a strong sense of compassion and connection to others, and solid, solid, counseling skills."

Jean Campbell—GED Counselor/GED Exam Administrator

Jean Campbell worked as a GED counselor with the school board of Broward County, Florida, for five years. She earned her B.A. in psychology at the University of Massachusetts, Boston, and her master's in education (M.Ed.) from Boston University.

GETTING STARTED

"My goal when studying for my master's degree was to go into mental health counseling and eventually get my doctorate in psychology. After I graduated with my master's degree, I moved from

Boston to Florida. At that time I had no luck finding a mental health counseling job, but a friend of a friend told me about the GED program. I made a phone call, set up an interview, and was hired on the spot. The director was impressed with my 'northern' education and had an immediate opening for a GED test administrator. The job required a master's degree. I did that for about six months, then was given more hours and moved into a GED counselor position. I worked for the school board for about five years, then moved into a mental health counseling position at a private agency."

WHAT THE WORK IS LIKE

"When I was a test administrator, the GED exam was given over a four-day period, for several hours in the morning. I worked with another administrator. We seated the students, took their entrance tickets and checked them against the roll we'd been given, read them the directions, handed out the tests, timed the various sections of the tests, then collected the exams and turned them into the GED office. We'd start all over again the next week with a new group of test takers.

"Basically, this particular job was more than boring. Of the four or so hours we were there each morning, three and a half of them were spent quietly waiting for the time to go by. I used to pass the time reading the test questions and seeing if I'd remembered all the math and science I'd learned in high school. I never understood why the job required you to have a master's degree.

"My work got more interesting when I was given a counseling position. The county had three GED counselors—I worked in the southern and central part of the county, another took the northern part, and the third was our supervisor.

"The GED preparation centers were spread out all over the county and used a variety of facilities: a storefront in a strip mall, a room in a church, the cafeteria of an old school. We even had centers in a prison and a half-way house.

"I worked between twenty-five to thirty hours and set my own schedule. I tried to visit each center at least once a month. I'd meet with students at each center and discuss with them their progress and their goals for after completing the GED exam. Some planned to enroll in the community college, some planned to go into technical schools, others had no real idea what they were going to do once they finished. It was my job to help them define their interests and let them know what options were available to them.

"Sometimes I worked with the students individually, sometimes in groups. They were all anxious about taking the GED exam, and I tried to encourage them and focus on what they'd do after the exam. My attitude was that their passing was a done deal— nothing to worry about. Let's just sort out what you'll do after that. I think they appreciated that."

THE UPSIDES
AND DOWNSIDES

"The job gave me a lot of freedom, with no one looking over my shoulder. The students were all appreciative of the attention and I enjoyed the interaction with them.

"Unfortunately, because there were so many centers to cover, I didn't get to follow up with too many of the students. By the time the month rotation had come around, many had left the prep program, taken the exam, and moved on. Often, I never heard if they passed or went on to enroll in a community college or technical program. Sometimes they'd come back to the center to let their instructor know how things had gone, but it was usually on a day when I wasn't there.

"Another downside to the job was the driving. I was always on the road, and I had no office space provided for me. My car and the trunk functioned as my office, and without a desk, it was hard to keep papers and files and supplies organized."

SALARIES

"I was paid straight hourly wages for both the testing and counseling jobs—around $19 an hour at the time. But the hours were never firm; I would be given between twenty-five to thirty a week, with no guarantees. So my income fluctuated a lot. I remember I had just purchased a new car and got my financing arranged based on the thirty hours a week I was working at the time. That very day my hours got cut to twenty-five.

"Plus, there were no benefits. No insurance or sick time or vacation days. Most of the staff resented that and it was bad for morale. They wouldn't give us forty hours to work, because then they'd have to provide the benefits, too, and they didn't want to do that."

ADVICE FROM JEAN CAMPBELL

"Working with adults can be very rewarding, especially seeing how happy they are when they've accomplished something and have goals they can continue to work toward. But I'd advise anyone to find a full-time job that provided benefits. Once you start working part-time for an agency, there's no guarantee that you will be given a full-time position. It often does happen in some settings, but check out first before you commit yourself to a long wait, that it can happen in the setting you're thinking of working for."

CHAPTER 6

ADULT EDUCATION ADMINISTRATION

Smooth operation of an educational institution or adult education program requires competent administrators. Education administrators provide direction, leadership, and day-to-day management of educational activities in schools, colleges and universities, community colleges, technical institutes, businesses, correctional institutions, museums, and job training and community service organizations.

Education administrators set educational standards and goals and aid in establishing policies and procedures to carry them out. They develop academic programs; train and motivate teachers and other staff; manage guidance and other student services; administer record keeping; prepare budgets; handle relations with parents, prospective students, employers, or others outside of education; and perform numerous other activities.

They supervise subordinate managers, management support staff, teachers, counselors, librarians, coaches, and others. In an organization such as a small day care center, there may be one administrator who handles all functions. In a major university or large school system, responsibilities are divided among many administrators, each with a specific function.

JOB TITLES AND DUTIES

Principals manage elementary and secondary schools. They set the academic tone as high-quality instruction is their main responsibility. Principals assign teachers and other staff, help them improve their skills, and evaluate them. They confer with them, advising, explaining, or answering procedural questions. They visit classrooms, review instructional objectives, and examine learning materials. They also meet with other administrators, students, parents, and representatives of community organizations. They prepare budgets and reports on various subjects, including finances, health, and attendance, and oversee the requisitioning and allocation of supplies. As school budgets become tighter, many principals are trying to encourage financial support for their schools from local businesses.

In recent years, as schools have become more involved with a student's emotional welfare as well as academic achievement, schools are providing more services to students. As a result, principals face new responsibilities. For example, in response to the growing number of dual-income and single-parent families and teenage parents, more schools have before- and after-school child care programs or family resource centers, which also may offer parenting classes and social service referrals. With the help of other community organizations, principals also may establish programs to combat the increase in crime, drug and alcohol abuse, and sexually transmitted disease among students.

Assistant principals aid the principal in the overall administration of the school. Depending on the number of students, a school may have more than one assistant principal, or may not have any. They are responsible for programming student classes and coordinating transportation, custodial, cafeteria, and other support services. They usually handle discipline, social and recreational programs, and health and safety. They also may counsel students on personal, educational, or vocational matters.

Central office administrators manage public schools in school district central offices. This group includes those who direct subject area programs such as English, music, vocational education, special education, and mathematics. They plan, evaluate, and improve curriculums and teaching techniques and help teachers improve their skills and learn about new methods and materials. They oversee career counseling programs and testing, which measures students' abilities and helps place them in appropriate classes.

Central office administrators also include directors of programs such as guidance, school psychology, athletics, curriculum and instruction, and professional development. With the trend toward site-based management, principals and assistant principals, along with teachers and other staff, have primary responsibility for many of these programs in their individual schools.

Academic deans, also known as deans of faculty, provosts, or university deans, are found in colleges and universities, assist presidents, and develop budgets and academic policies and programs. They direct and coordinate activities of deans of individual colleges and chairpersons of academic departments.

College or university department heads or chairpersons are in charge of departments such as English, biological science, or mathematics. They coordinate schedules of classes and teaching assignments, propose budgets, recruit, interview, and hire applicants for teaching positions, evaluate faculty members, and perform other administrative duties in addition to teaching.

Deans of students, also known as vice presidents of student affairs or student life, or directors of student services, direct and coordinate admissions, foreign student services, and health and counseling services, as well as social, recreation, and related programs. In a small college, they may counsel students.

Registrars are custodians of students' education records. They register students, prepare student transcripts, evaluate academic records, oversee the preparation of college catalogs and schedules of classes, and analyze registration statistics.

Directors of admissions manage the process of recruiting and admitting students and work closely with financial aid directors, who oversee scholarship, fellowship, and loan programs.

Directors of student activities plan and arrange social, cultural, and recreational activities, assist student-run organizations, and may orient new students. Athletic directors plan and direct intramural and intercollegiate athletic activities, including publicity for athletic events, preparation of budgets, and supervision of coaches.

WORKING CONDITIONS

Education administrators hold management positions with significant responsibility. Coordinating and interacting with faculty, parents, and students can be fast-paced and stimulating, but also stressful and demanding. Some jobs include travel.

Principals and assistant principals whose main duty is discipline may find working with difficult students frustrating, but challenging.

Most education administrators work more than forty hours a week, including many nights and weekends when school activities take place. Unlike teachers, they usually work year-round.

EMPLOYMENT FIGURES

Education administrators hold about 390,000 jobs nationwide. About nine out of ten work in educational services—in elementary, secondary, and technical schools and colleges and universities. The rest work in child day care centers, religious organizations, job training centers, state departments of education, and businesses and other organizations that provide training for their employees.

THE QUALIFICATIONS YOU'LL NEED

Education administrator is not usually an entry-level job. Many education administrators begin their careers in related occupations and prepare for a job in education administration by completing a master's or doctoral degree in administration or adult education. Because of the diversity of duties and levels of responsibility, their educational backgrounds and experience vary considerably.

Principals, assistant principals, central office administrators, and academic deans usually have taught or held another related job before moving into administration. Some teachers move directly into principalships; however, most first gain experience as an assistant principal or in a central office administrative job.

ADVANCEMENT OPPORTUNITIES

In some cases, top administrators move up from related staff jobs such as recruiter, program director, career placement counselor, or financial aid or admissions counselor. Earning a higher degree generally improves one's advancement opportunities in education administration.

To be considered for education administrator positions, workers must first prove themselves in their current jobs. In evaluating candidates, supervisors look for determination, confidence, innovativeness, motivation, and managerial attributes, such as ability to make sound decisions and to organize and coordinate work efficiently.

Since much of an administrator's job involves interacting with others—from students to parents to teachers to the community at large—they must have strong interpersonal skills and be effective communicators and motivators. Knowledge of management principles and practices, gained through work experience and formal education, is important.

In public schools, principals, assistant principals, and school administrators in central offices generally need a master's degree in education administration or educational supervision and a state teaching certificate. Some principals and central office administrators have a doctorate in education administration.

In private schools, they often have a master's or doctoral degree, but may hold only a bachelor's degree since they are not subject to state certification requirements.

Academic deans usually have a doctorate in their specialty. Admissions, student affairs, and financial aid directors and registrars often start in related staff jobs with bachelor's degrees—any field usually is acceptable—and get advanced degrees in college student affairs or higher education administration. A Ph.D. or Ed.D. usually is necessary for top student affairs positions.

Computer literacy and a background in mathematics or statistics may be assets in admissions, records, and financial work.

Advanced degrees in higher education administration, educational supervision, and college student affairs are offered in many colleges and universities. The National Council for Accreditation of Teacher Education accredits programs. Education administration degree programs include courses in school management, school law, school finance and budgeting, curriculum development and evaluation, research design and data analysis, community relations, politics in education, counseling, and leadership.

Educational supervision degree programs include courses in supervision of instruction and curriculum, human relations, curriculum development, research, and advanced pedagogy courses.

Education administrators advance by moving up an administrative ladder or transferring to larger schools or systems. They also may become superintendent of a school system or president of an educational institution.

JOB OUTLOOK

Substantial competition is expected for prestigious jobs as adult education administrators. Many faculty and other staff meet the education and experience requirements for these jobs, and seek promotion. However, the number of openings is relatively small; only the most highly qualified are selected. Candidates who have the most formal education and who are willing to relocate should have the best job prospects.

On the other hand, it is becoming more difficult to attract candidates for principal, vice principal, and administration jobs at the elementary and secondary school level—competition for these jobs is declining. Many teachers no longer have an incentive to move into these positions since the pay is not significantly higher and does not compensate for the added workload and responsibility of the position. Also, site-based management has given teachers more decision-making responsibility in recent years, possibly satisfying their desire to move into administration.

Employment of education administrators is expected to grow about as fast as the average for all occupations over the 1996–2006 period. However, most job openings will result from the need to replace administrators who retire or transfer to other occupations.

School enrollments at the elementary, secondary, and postsecondary level are all expected to grow over the projection period. Rather than opening new schools, many existing school populations will expand, spurring demand for assistant principals to help with the increased workload. Employment of education administrators will also grow as more services are provided to students and as efforts to improve the quality of education continue.

However, budget constraints are expected to moderate growth in this profession. At the postsecondary level, some institutions have been reducing administrative staffs to contain costs. Some colleges are consolidating administrative jobs and contracting with other providers for some administrative functions.

SALARIES

Salaries of education administrators vary according to position, level of responsibility and experience, and the size and location of the institution.

According to a survey of public schools, conducted by the Educational Research Service, average salaries for principals and assistant principals in the 1996–97 school year (the most recent figures available) were as follows:

Principals:

Elementary school	$62,900
Junior high/middle school	66,900
Senior high school	72,400

Assistant principals:

Elementary school	$52,300
Junior high/middle school	56,500
Senior high school	59,700

Salaries for directors, managers, coordinators, and supervisors of instructional services were $70,800.

According to the College and University Personnel Association, median annual salaries for selected administrators in higher education are as follows:

Academic deans:

Medicine	$201,200
Law	141,400
Engineering	112,800
Arts and sciences	82,500
Business	81,700
Education	80,000
Social sciences	61,800
Mathematics	59,900

Student services directors:

Admissions and registrar	$50,700
Student financial aid	45,400
Student activities	34,500

FIRSTHAND ACCOUNTS

The firsthand accounts that follow in this chapter include an education supervisor in a correctional facility, a computer learning center coordinator, and an assistant to the supervisor of adult education in a career and technology center.

Bernard Lopinto—Education Supervisor

Bernard LoPinto is currently an education supervisor at Mid-Orange Correctional Facility in Warwick, New York. He was a correctional educator for twelve years until his recent promotion to supervisor.

He earned his B.A. in English from St. John's University in New York City in 1969 and his M.A. in reading from Hofstra University, Hempstead, New York, in 1973. In 1997 he received a Certificate of Advanced Study in Education Administration from State University of New York at Cortland.

GETTING STARTED

"I became involved in correctional education by accident. I was unemployed for over a year—unable to find a teaching position in public school. My seventeen years of experience made me too expensive for school districts to want to hire me. Desperate, I went into a New York State Employment Service office, determined to find something I could do in civil service. That's when I found the listing for teachers in correctional facilities. I sent in my information and, within a few months, had a position at a nearby state facility.

"I became interested in the administrative end when I transferred to a facility that was just opening up. Most of the other teachers in the new facility did not have as much experience as I did, and I became an unofficial trainer, especially to those who seemed to be having problems with discipline and classroom management—areas where I feel quite competent. When I saw how a teacher's life could improve with a little instruction, and how a better trained teacher could change an entire class, I decided I wanted to teach teachers and started working toward administrative certification.

"Besides my experience as a public school teacher and my graduate work in reading, my training as a correctional educator has been all on-the-job. I owe my knowledge to my colleagues who showed me the ropes, to the Department of Corrections training program, and to my students who broke me in without mercy.

"I took my training in education administration at State University of New York at Cortland between 1992 and 1997. During this time, I took the civil service test for Education Supervisor. After three years on the promotions list, I was hired as a supervisor by my present facility."

WHAT THE WORK IS LIKE

"Our students are adult, male inmates. They are enrolled by requirements of the NYS Department of Correctional Services.

Inmates with reading and math levels below 5.0 on the Test of Adult Basic Education (TABE) are required to attend classes all day. Inmates scoring below 8.0 on the TABE are required to attend school half-days. Inmates scoring at 8.0 in reading and math are permitted to attend a voluntary GED class at night.

"I am new to this position, and this particular position has been vacant for four years. One of the problems in correctional education is that budgetary considerations often override the educational needs of inmates.

"There is too much to do for my job to be boring. It's a forty-hour week in an atmosphere that feels crowded and cramped. What passes for my office is a cubby hole at the end of a hallway. We are in the process of reconfiguring an empty classroom for a new office.

"My day starts at eight o'clock, and soon there are inmates waiting to see me to help them find old GED records or to complain about their class or their teacher. I help with education records, but I do not entertain complaints. Inmates can be quite manipulative, and the best way to deal with manipulation is to cut it off early. Monday morning is also the day we run program committee, the body that makes sure every inmate in the facility is in some kind of work or education program. Right now we have over forty inmates on a waiting list for school. Part of my job is to program as many as possible into some kind of class. As soon as an opening occurs in a class, I have to fill it.

"Between inmate problems, teacher problems, and directions from my supervisor, the deputy superintendent of programs, I don't get too much time to sit down."

THE UPSIDES

"I most like that I have the authority to make the changes necessary to the running of the school, and I think my presence has been a positive influence. I have already been able to make small

changes—remove hats in the building, no loitering in the halls—
that have improved the learning atmosphere."

THE DOWNSIDES

"I regret that I have to spend so much time in management activities that I haven't had time to be the instructional leader I want to
be. A new GED exam is coming, and the New York State Education
Department has mandated new learning standards for adult education. These standards are not yet being met in our school, and I want
to help my teachers meet them. I expect to start a staff development
program to meet these challenges within the next few months."

SALARIES

"In New York State, a correctional educator at the top of the
scale can expect to earn about $10,000 or more a year less than a
public school teacher. My research has shown me that this is common throughout the country.

"The pay in New York starts in the mid-twenties and ends in the
low forties. Supervisors at the top of the scale earn about 12 percent more than teachers at top pay."

ADVICE FROM BERNARD LOPINTO

"More than anything else, education is what keeps people from
returning to prison. This knowledge is what motivates me most.
We may be an individual's last chance to stay free and society's
last chance to stay safe.

"Correctional educators need to be people managers who are
able to recognize when someone is trying to manipulate them.
That is the biggest danger—manipulation by inmates.

"At the same time, we need to be sensitive to the educational
and emotional needs of our students. These are people to whom
school is the scene of many failures, and we want to help them
find some success.

"Some background in special education would be helpful. Many of our students have undiagnosed learning disabilities, and there are few special education programs in correctional education.

"Most correctional education jobs are civil service, so a teacher interested in breaking in (no pun intended) should start there."

Terry Thompson—Computer Learning Center Coordinator

Terry Thompson is the Computer Learning Center Coordinator at Independence, Inc., an Independent Living Center in Lawrence, Kansas. He started there in 1994.

He earned his B.A. in psychology, from Purdue University in W. Lafayette, Indiana, in 1986.

GETTING STARTED

"My bachelor's degree was in psychology. I worked for a while in psychology research, but that was a grant-funded position that ultimately ended. To survive, I ended up working in a corporate computing position for several years, all the while seeking a more meaningful way to contribute my talents to improving people's lives. In my present position, I have found a nearly perfect marriage between my psychology training, my computer knowledge, and my desire to help others.

"I applied for this job with a strong professional background and good communication skills, but lacking some of the preferred, if not required, qualifications, such as a knowledge of computer-based assistive technologies for persons with disabilities, and experience working with persons with disabilities. I must have made up for these deficits with my passion, because I genuinely wanted this job and wanted to help others in any way I could to live meaningful, independent lives. I must have adequately conveyed this passion in my job interview."

"Independence, Inc., receives funding to provide services to persons with disabilities, whether their disabilities are physical, mental, or cognitive. The Computer Learning Center is one program within the larger organization. We serve an average of fifty students per month. Most are adults of working age. About 75 percent of these students claim that improved job marketability is their primary reason for seeking computer training.

"The philosophy that governs independent living centers is that persons with disabilities are free to make their own choices. Our training system embodies this philosophy, as each student declares a formal goal or goals upon entering a path of study, then receives whatever training may be appropriate for them to attain this goal. The training, in other words, is very individualized. We provide some formal classes, but much of the training is through students' working independently toward attaining the goals they've set. The only requirements are occasional prerequisites (knowledge or completed classes) for certain intermediate or advanced lines of study.

"Often the students' goals are to find employment utilizing their new computer skills. Other students may just be looking to establish an e-mail account or to learn how to efficiently locate information on the Internet.

"As coordinator of the Computer Learning Center, I am responsible for all facets of program management, including student counseling, student goal planning and tracking, budget management, marketing, outreach, curriculum development, teaching, and staff hiring and supervision. There is no specific routine that directs my day. Instead, I usually make a list of those tasks that need to be done, prioritize them, and outline a proposed itinerary for the week. I have learned it is very difficult to adhere strictly to a specific schedule; problems with students, the staff that I supervise, or the computers in the computer lab, often surface without notice. These problems often demand immediate attention, and the tasks that I had originally designated as top priority for that day get tossed to the back burner. The exceptions are scheduled tasks that involve other people, such as meetings with other agency staff members, meetings or presentations within the community, or previously scheduled appointments with students. I very rarely cancel or reschedule appointments. If an emergency situation arises prior to such an event, I exercise as much skill as possible to delegate an appropriate response to other capable staff or diffuse the situation, at least temporarily, if not entirely, so I can get to my scheduled appointment.

"Despite the hectic schedule, most of the duties I perform are all interesting and intrinsically rewarding, which makes it all worthwhile.

"Instructors' job descriptions in the computer lab are much more clearly defined. They assist students, either by teaching formal classes on particular topics or helping as needed with students who are studying independently. About 40 percent of my job is direct training similar to that provided by instructors. The remainder is spent with those administrative duties described above. All of this generally happens between 8:00 A.M. and 5:00 P.M. Very little overtime is required. That's where prioritization comes in. I may never get some tasks accomplished, but that's okay as long as I accomplish those tasks that are most critical."

THE UPSIDES

"I try not to dwell on what is satisfying or not satisfying about my work. When there is something to be done, I do it. Each moment brings new challenges, and each moment old challenges are met. If I take time to assess whether I like or dislike what I'm doing, then I'm not actually engaged in doing that task. So I don't think in this way.

"With that said, if I am wrestled into declaring satisfying aspects of my job, I would say that the entire job is satisfying because everything I do will directly benefit another person. Often I know and work closely with the recipients of these benefits, and I am strengthened by watching them grow and by receiving their positive feedback. I did not have this same level of satisfaction working in the corporate world."

THE DOWNSIDES

"If I am wrestled into declaring dissatisfying aspects of my job, I would say that the distractions mentioned above can be intrusive and annoying unless one expects them and appreciates them as part of the workday.

"Co-workers often express some dissatisfaction with salaries, as employees at not-for-profit social service agencies tend to earn less than they could with the same skills in a for-profit environment. As a person who left the for-profit world for the not-for-profit, I have a greater appreciation for the intrinsic rewards associated with helping others."

SALARIES

"I started at around $29,000 and have worked my way up to $30,000 after five years. To my knowledge, there have never been any raises at this organization beyond cost of living increases. I am one of the highest paid people on our staff, and many of my co-workers are at poverty level.

"However, we also have several people on staff who have been here for more than ten years! This is testimony to the reward than can be found in meaningful work. In my previous (corporate) position, where raises were given much more liberally, but the work was much less meaningful, the average length of stay was four years, and nobody on a staff of fifty was even close to the ten-year mark."

ADVICE FROM TERRY THOMPSON

"This line of work—computer training for persons with disabilities—is unique. Jobs are not plentiful, though there are related jobs that are more common, such as special education teachers or directors, occupational therapists, physical therapists, and jobs within disabled student services departments at colleges or universities.

"I entered into the field through psychology, life experience, and strange luck. I recommend that others who are interested in working with assistive technology and/or with persons with disabilities focus on any of the above mentioned disciplines and receive as high a degree as possible within these disciplines.

"Most reasonable-paying jobs in this area will require administrative or managerial skills. I encourage all interested people to seek supervisory and managerial experience wherever you can. Always seek new responsibilities in everything you do. If your knowledge base is diverse, and if you are dedicated and hardworking, these qualities will be recognized, and if you are not promoted in your present position, you will at least be building your resume. If a person hopes to earn a reasonable living in social services, he or she will have to develop these administrative qualities."

Debi Violante—Assistant to the Supervisor of Adult Education

Debi Violante is the assistant to the supervisor of adult education at the Lancaster County Career and Technology Center in Lancaster, Pennsylvania. She has gained her expertise through a variety of computer and continuing education courses. She has been at this job since 1998.

GETTING STARTED

"I consider myself a lifelong learner; I became interested in the school first as a prospective student. As luck would have it, a phone call for more information about the courses offered at the school led to a conversation about how I was looking for a job and the supervisor was looking for an assistant.

"My training was 100 percent on-the-job. The adult education supervisor showed me the procedures for the numerous tasks that must be completed on a daily basis, as well as gave me an overview of the department's mission. On one occasion, someone who does the same job at one of the school's other campuses came by to give me one full day of training. My computer skills and previous customer service experience, combined with my ability to multitask, are my best qualifications."

WHAT THE WORK IS LIKE

"A lot of our students are people who have been downsized from a position they have held for a long time. Once unemployed, they are painfully aware of the skills needed to compete in the current job market, or that they need to update skills they already have. We get a lot of women interested in bettering themselves, hoping to possibly find part-time work around their current job of being a Mom.

"We also have people interested in a career change, or young adults who have no college background, but who are interested in a career, not just a job.

"There is little that is boring about my position as assistant to the supervisor of adult ed. A typical day begins before I even get there; there are several voice-mail messages waiting for me when I arrive at 9:00 A.M., and the first thing I do is note them, gather the necessary information, then return the calls. Most of these calls are from people wanting more information about the courses we offer, and I spend a good amount of time describing the content, cost, hours, and benefits to the prospective student. We have a printed catalog that we mail to anyone who has an interest, but I've found that people prefer to hear a friendly voice elaborate on the information contained in our catalog. Calls of this nature continue coming in for the entire day and can sometimes impede the other work I need to accomplish, but they are the lifeblood of the school, making them a priority.

"The ability to work on many different tasks at one time is essential because, in addition to personal contact with prospective students on the phone and in the office, there are currently enrolled students who will visit—without warning—needing my assistance. They may want to check the status of their Pell Grant, student loan, or other source of funding; they could have a question concerning the most recent invoice they received, or they might need the answer to a school scheduling question. Sometimes, they just stop by trying to get me to donate blood (our health department), or buy cheesecake for a fund-raiser. I enjoy getting to know the students and like that I am able to greet them by their names when they come by.

"In my position, it is important to gain a grasp of school policies concerning just about anything having to do with classes, students, and payments. Complete records are kept in a traditional filing system, as well as in spreadsheet and database format on the PC. Any money that comes in or is paid out of the adult education budget must be accounted for promptly, which isn't always easy when twenty-five people have called the school requesting information about any of the full-time programs (about a dozen) or the short-term evening courses (more than one hundred between three campuses) we offer to adults.

"The ability to prioritize is important, yet it can be lost when the day takes on a different set of priorities on its own. As an assistant, I need to be available to assist with whatever project my supervisor is working on (e.g., new classes starting or classes canceled due to under-enrollment, letters or grant proposals needing to be typed on the PC, brainstorming for new ways to handle the volumes of data needing to be stored, etc.).

"Many times, I find myself frustrated by the inability to secure some quiet time to accomplish what was on my to do list. I will leave at 5:00 P.M. remembering only what I have not done, not what kept me busy for eight hours.

"In addition to the daily administrative work, projects, and personal contact, I am also responsible for helping the director of adult education, as well as the director of curriculum for the school and the tech prep coordinator with various word processing assignments. Budget restrictions not only keep my salary comparable to that of someone working at a fast-food restaurant, but prohibit the hiring of an executive secretary for these important people at the school."

THE UPSIDES

"The most rewarding part of working in adult education is the feeling I get after I've helped someone. For instance, I once spoke to an older man who had lost a long-held job after his company downsized. He was interested in taking computer courses since he discovered how necessary they are in today's market.

"After talking for a few minutes, it was evident that this man was quite intelligent, and I learned that he had been quite successful in marketing before losing his job. Unfortunately, he had not been able to find a position comparable to the one he'd left; we speculated that his age may have had something to do with it. It broke my heart to learn that he was working in a department store and supplementing his income by drawing from his retirement money. He wasn't terribly excited about learning so many new skills to secure employment until I mentioned an organization that would pay for his education because he was a displaced worker. I could hear the hope in his voice, and by the way he thanked me, one would think that *I* had offered to pay for his schooling. Experiences such as this one are extremely gratifying and are not uncommon in adult ed."

THE DOWNSIDES

"Most definitely, the worst part about working in adult education is the constraint of a budget that does not recognize the need to compensate the skills they require for such a position. As a recently widowed mother of three, I need to earn enough money to support my family, but because I cannot, I am currently looking elsewhere for employment. I regret having to make this decision, because I have come to appreciate the joys of helping adults improve their lives and enjoy interacting with so many of the people I work with on a daily basis.

"The Department of Education has excellent benefits, but employees pay into them and have a mandatory amount withdrawn from each paycheck, which is deposited toward a (matched) retirement plan. There is no reward for providing above-average work, and the system provides a cost of living raise annually whether we are poor workers or excellent. An employee whose work is not acceptable will be let go, but if their performance is good enough to keep their job, they get the raise just like everyone else. There is also little room for advancement, which can result in diminishing one's motivation."

SALARIES

"Currently, I earn $7.50 an hour, which reflects a fifty cent an hour raise from my $7.00 starting salary. After my sixty-day probationary period, the raise was automatic, assuming they didn't fire me. I can look forward to a raise of about another twenty-five cents an hour at the end of the fiscal year, but I will not see it until the end of the calendar year.

"Our salaries are based on a thirty-seven-and-a-half-hour work-week, allowing for a thirty-minute lunch break each day."

ADVICE FROM DEBI VIOLANTE

"For people interested in adult education administration work, I would suggest they examine their motives and their own personality; patience is important—with yourself and with the expectations of your superiors.

"When I say to examine your motives, I am addressing the salary issue. I think it is important to realize there is a ceiling and how close that ceiling is to your head.

"Computer training is essential, as well as the ability to handle multiple priorities, pay attention to detail, and communicate effectively in person and on the phone."

SOURCES FOR MORE INFORMATION

General information on adult education is available from:

American Association for Adult and Continuing Education
1200 Nineteenth Street NW, Suite 300
Washington, DC 20036

American Vocational Association
1410 King Street
Alexandria, VA 22314

ERIC Clearinghouse on Adult, Career, and Vocational Education
1900 Kenny Road
Columbus, OH 43210-1090

ERIC Clearinghouse on Rural Education and Small Schools
P. O. Box 1348
Charleston, WV 25325-1348

U.S. Department of Education
Office of Vocational and Adult Education
Washington, DC 20202

ABE

Information on adult basic education programs and teacher certification requirements is available from state departments of education and local school districts.

Vocational-Technical

For information about adult vocational-technical education teaching positions, contact state departments of vocational-technical education.

Continuing Education

For information on adult continuing education teaching positions, contact departments of local government, state adult education departments, schools, colleges and universities, religious organizations, and a wide range of businesses that provide formal training for their employees.

TESOL

Information on teaching English as a second language and on job openings is available from:

Teachers of English to Speakers of Other Languages, Inc. (TESOL)
1600 Cameron Street, Suite 300
Alexandria, VA 22314-2705

GED

For information on the GED, contact:

American Council on Education
One Dupont Circle NW
Washington DC, 20036

School Teaching

Information on licensure or certification requirements and approved teacher training institutions is available from local school systems and state departments of education.

Information on teachers' unions and education-related issues may be obtained from:

American Federation of Teachers
555 New Jersey Avenue NW
Washington, DC 20001

National Education Association
1201 Sixteenth Street NW
Washington, DC 20036

A list of institutions with accredited teacher education programs can be obtained from:

National Council for Accreditation of Teacher Education
2010 Massachusetts Avenue NW, Suite 500
Washington, DC 20036

For information on voluntary national teacher certification requirements, contact:

National Board for Professional Teaching Standards
26555 Evergreen Road, Suite 400
Southfield, MI 48076

Counseling

For general information about counseling, as well as information on specialties such as school, college, mental health, rehabilitation, multicultural, career, marriage and family, and gerontological counseling, contact:

American Counseling Association
5999 Stevenson Avenue
Alexandria, VA 22304

For information on accredited counseling and related training programs, contact:

Council for Accreditation of Counseling and Related Educational
    Programs

American Counseling Association
5999 Stevenson Avenue
Alexandria, VA 22304

For information on national certification requirements for counselors, contact:

National Board for Certified Counselors
3 Terrace Way, Suite D
Greensboro, NC 27403

For information on certification requirements for rehabilitation counselors and a list of accredited rehabilitation education programs, contact:

Council on Rehabilitation Counselor Certification
1835 Rohlwing Road, Suite E
Rolling Meadows, IL 60008

State departments of education can supply information on colleges and universities that offer approved guidance and counseling training for state certification and licensure requirements. State employment service offices have information about job opportunities and entrance requirements for counselors.

Administration

For information on elementary and secondary school principals, assistant principals, and central office administrators, contact:

American Federation of School Administrators
1729 Twenty-First Street NW
Washington, DC 20009

American Association of School Administrators
1801 North Moore Street
Arlington, VA 22209

For information on elementary school principals and assistant principals, contact:

The National Association of Elementary School Principals
1615 Duke Street
Alexandria, VA 22314-3483

For information on secondary school principals and assistant principals, contact:

The National Association of Secondary School Principals
1904 Association Drive
Reston, VA 20191

For information on college student affairs administrators, contact:

National Association of Student Personnel Administrators
1875 Connecticut Avenue NW, Suite 418
Washington, DC 20009-5728

For information on collegiate registrars and admissions officers, contact:

American Association of Collegiate Registrars and Admissions Officers
One Dupont Circle NW, Suite 330
Washington, DC 20036-1171